THE
PROMISE
AND PERIL OF
ENVIRONMENTAL
JUSTICE

THE
PROMISE
AND PERIL OF
ENVIRONMENTAL
JUSTICE

CHRISTOPHER H. FOREMAN JR.

BROOKINGS INSTITUTION PRESS
Washington, D.C.

Library of Congress Cataloging-in-Publication data

Foreman, Christopher H.
    The promise and peril of environmental justice / Christopher H.
Foreman Jr.
    p. cm.
    Includes bibliographical references.
    ISBN 0-8157-2878-6 (cloth)
    1. Environmental degradation—United States. 2. Environmental
policy—United States. 3. Environmental justice—United States. I.
Title.

GE150 .F67 1998
363.7'00973—ddc21   98-25431
                                                                 CIP

9 8 7 6 5 4 3 2 1

The paper used in this publication meets minimum requirements of the American
National Standard for Information Sciences—Permanence of Paper for Printed Library
Materials: ANSI Z39.48-1984.

Typeset in Palatino

Composition by R. Lynn Rivenbark
Macon, Georgia

Printed by
R. R. Donnelley and Sons
Harrisonburg, Virginia

To Thelma P. Foreman
mother, believer, and skeptic

FOREWORD

THE PAST THREE DECADES of environmental advocacy and policymaking have witnessed much success, including several landmark laws and significant environmental improvement. But environmental policymaking is today more complex and demanding than ever, due partly to changes in the advocacy milieu. During the first Earth Day celebration in April 1970, equity was a barely visible theme. Today both policymakers and a well-established environmental movement must grapple with impassioned demands that "environmental justice" be accorded low-income and minority citizens. President Clinton has instructed federal agencies to demonstrate due sensitivity and responsiveness.

In this timely and provocative volume Christopher H. Foreman Jr., a senior fellow in the Brookings Governmental Studies program, assesses the opportunities and pitfalls attending the new emphasis on equitable environmental policy. He challenges both the empirical basis of environmental justice claims and the belief that advocacy effectively pursues the health and economic interests of targeted communities. While acknowledging that genuine social grievances undergird the environmental justice movement, Foreman prompts us to reconsider whether that movement, or the administrative innovation that has resulted, can effectively address those grievances. He argues that while activists are winning the political battle for attention to the issue of environmental justice, the very nature of activism substantially complicates the search for responsive policies. Foreman suggests that a political rhetoric of risk and racism often misconstrues the challenge of enhancing both collective health and neighborhood livability. He therefore outlines an alternative, though demanding, pathway for future debate and institution building.

The author wishes to thank several persons who read all or part of the manuscript. They include Michael Gough, John A. Hird, John Kingdon, Marcel LaFollette, Marc Landy, Thomas E. Mann, Howard Margolis, Barry Rabe, Jeffrey K. Stine, James Q. Wilson, and James B. Witkin. Fawn Johnson, Stephanianna Lozito, and Carole Plowfield served as primary research assistants on the project. Additional research assistance was provided by Amy Finkelstein, Yaron Glazer, Azadeh Moaveni, Jennifer Pennell, and Josh Steinitz.

The manuscript was edited by Kerry Kern and verified by Matthew Atlas. Sherry Smith provided the index, and Sally Martin proofed the pages.

The views expressed here are solely those of the author and should not be ascribed to the persons whose assistance is acknowledged above or to the trustees, officers, or other staff members of the Brookings Institution.

MICHAEL H. ARMACOST
President

July 1998
Washington, D.C.

CONTENTS

THE
PROMISE
AND PERIL OF
ENVIRONMENTAL
JUSTICE

1

CHALLENGES

Americans overwhelmingly deplore both racial discrimination and environmental degradation, but until recently these concerns seldom directly intersected in public policy discourse. Throughout the 1960s and 1970s environmentalists attended to an agenda far removed from racial minorities and the poor. Although environmentalists as individuals often sympathized with, and even actively supported, the political struggles of ethnic minorities (and African Americans in particular), environmentalism and civil rights/social welfare evolved as distinct issue spheres, each with its own statutory framework, institutions, and audiences. Environmentalism, especially at the national level, had little racial aspect as such.

Today the environmental decisions of business and government alike are widely recognized as having potentially serious equity implications, especially for minority and low-income communities. Environmentalists, community representatives, and policymakers address this new blend of concerns under three labels: environmental racism; environmental equity; and, most recently, environmental justice. The core claim of the environmental justice movement is that

1

a variety of environmental burdens (for example, toxic waste sites, polluted air and water, dirty jobs, underenforcement of environmental laws) have fallen disproportionately on low-income persons and communities of color. A related claim, or frequent presumption, is that health risks associated with pollution have likewise been borne disproportionately by such persons and communities.

Government at every level is being pressed to address environmental justice. Not surprisingly, the most visible and broad-gauged response has emerged in Washington. Soon after becoming administrator of the Environmental Protection Agency (EPA) in 1993, Carol Browner announced her intention to build on the commitment of her predecessor to address possible sources of environmental inequity. And in February 1994 President Bill Clinton issued executive order 12898, an ambitious proclamation instructing federal agencies to integrate environmental justice into their ongoing missions (see Appendix A).

Most writing about environmental justice has had at least one of two aims, and sometimes both. One purpose is political agenda-setting. Activists and journalists have tried to dramatize and legitimize environmental justice as a problem by drawing attention to examples of local environments that have received short shrift from the political and economic system. This activist literature approvingly recounts tales of communities mobilizing against an array of hazardous conditions and unwanted facilities.[1] Community energies are driven largely by residents' belief that adverse health effects either have already appeared (due to past or present pollution) or could appear in the future (if new pollution sources are created or if existing ones are either enhanced or ignored). A second focus in the literature is empirical enlightenment. Some analysts—including both activists and more dispassionate observers, often employing quantitative techniques—have attempted to ask: How much environmental injustice or inequity is there?[2] Some commentators, perhaps most notably sociologist Robert Bullard, have played interchangeable advocacy and analytic roles. In a substantial series of publications since the 1980s Bullard argues that significant (and especially race-based) inequity has often prevailed in the distribution of environmental burdens and benefits. This state of affairs, according to Bullard, justifies fundamental policy reform grounded in what he calls an "environmental justice paradigm."[3]

This essay aims neither to promote environmental justice as a political cause nor to measure (if such a thing is possible) the current extent of injustice. Instead, the purpose here is to assess emerging prospects for environmental justice as a federal policy initiative. It will be argued here that the federal enterprise is beset by a number of difficult challenges:

—Empirical support for claims of disproportionate pollution impacts and discriminatory regulatory enforcement is actually much weaker than environmental justice advocates usually admit. In the foreseeable future, the EPA and Congress will probably lack strong scientific justification for major policy change on this front.

—Environmental justice is driven by aspirations for community empowerment, for social justice, and for public health, which federal policy will find difficult to address effectively using environmental means.

—Environmental justice advocacy probably directs community attention away from those problems posing the greatest risks and may therefore have the ironic effect of undermining public health in precisely those communities it endeavors to help.

—If pursued aggressively, environmental justice may exacerbate aspects of environmental policymaking that have been widely bemoaned (such as economic inefficiency, muddled policy priorities, the gap between expert and public perceptions of risk, and local inflexibility on siting issues).

—Federal environmental justice faces significant political hurdles. These include: the lack of congressional support, the primacy of states and localities in siting issues generally, and the infeasibility of what would otherwise be an obvious policy response—a ban on new siting in and near low-income communities and communities of color.

The limitations and drawbacks of environmental justice are seldom discussed, partly because little natural constituency exists for such discussion. This is especially true of two subtle but fundamental aspects of the environmental justice movement: (1) its chronic and institutionally rooted inability to define and pursue a coherent set of environmental policy priorities, and (2) its unwillingness to face politically inconvenient facts about environmental health risks.

Environmental justice is multifaceted—part racialized environmental populism, part public health anxiety, and part social justice advocacy—but it shares much with the larger milieu in which it operates. Its ultimate roots lie in the eternal yearning for a more democratic and egalitarian society comprised of livable communities. The phenomenon is directly fueled largely by the same grassroots antitoxics sentiments and NIMBY (not in my back yard) impulses that have pervaded post-1980 environmentalism. Not surprisingly, environmental justice activists generally reject the NIMBY label as pejorative. They shun as inherently unjust any displacement of hazards from some citizens onto others. Real justice, it is believed, requires the elimination of hazards.

Nevertheless the NIMBY shoe often fits. Even Lois Gibbs (famous for her leading role as neighborhood organizer at Love Canal and later head of the Citizens Clearinghouse for Hazardous Waste) admits that "for the vast majority of groups in the Movement, the local fight is everything."[4] Local residents certainly do not wish to victimize other communities by displacing pollution onto them. Yet the hard political reality is that mobilization occurs most readily because of a personal and collective interest in opposing specific perceived threats in a particular locale. Neither preventing the displacement of that threat onto others, nor the more nebulous desire for a more just society, can possibly have the same galvanizing effect on ordinary citizens.

Although activists often stress differences between minority and nonminority communities, the similarities are far more striking. There is generally little detectable difference between minority and nonminority neighborhoods regarding the fundamental sentiments and objectives that motivate challenges to siting and demands for aggressive cleanups (and sometimes even neighborhood relocation). Minority communities, like others, have strong incentives to demand "gold-plated" cleanups of waste sites and costly relocations. The reason is that entities other than the community typically bear the major cost. Indeed, as environmental policy currently functions neither minority nor nonminority communities need face tradeoffs among risk abatement expenditures.[5]

For whites and minorities alike, there exists a clash between a communitarian language on the one hand and the managerial and pluralist languages common among other (often more powerful) stakeholders in, and critics of, environmental policy on the other.[6] Where the managerial and pluralist languages stress, respectively, scientific expertise and the play of group interests as legitimating forces in policymaking, the communitarian alternative espouses direct citizen action and influence. Both minority and nonminority citizens exhibit similar suspicions of experts who often downplay hazards that residents deem significant.[7] Both are likewise often suspicious of industry.[8] And both environmental justice and the broader phenomenon of environmental populism, sometimes referred to as "ecopopulism," are ultimately less concerned with health risks than with advocacy itself—the elevation of a distinctive *community* voice whenever and wherever possible in the environmental policy process.[9] Though the specter of mass poisoning is a powerful theme for mobilizing and advocacy, anxiety about health is largely subordinate to the democratic objective of enabling citizens to hold public institutions accountable and private capital at bay.

Environmental justice also provides a rubric under which to reiterate familiar economic redistributive claims and to propose new avenues of redress. In the latter vein we observe EPA and other agencies, including the federal Department of Housing and Urban Development, collaborating on the ambitious "brownfields" economic redevelopment initiative. Brownfields are abandoned or underutilized parcels of land, lightly contaminated from previous industrial activity, that do not qualify as priority cleanup sites because they do not pose a serious health risk. At the community level, redistributive aims are most clearly apparent in the larger agendas, and even the names, of grassroots organizations; consider, for example, the Southwest Network for Environmental and

Economic Justice, or the Environmental Justice Project of the Southern Organizing Committee for Economic and Social Justice. In addition to (or perhaps instead of) the overt claim that low-income persons and people of color lack adequate wealth and power—a claim to which the American political and economic regime exhibits a decidedly limited responsiveness—environmental justice takes a slightly different tack that, advocates hope, offers additional political leverage over the underlying social disparities that most concern them. Environmental justice argues that an increased role for grassroots voices, combined with an environmentalism more sensitive to economic injustices, will tend to be protective of health in affected communities. Environmental justice announces: "We too often live and work near unpleasant and possibly dangerous sites and materials. We deserve a reduction in the conditions that make this happen." Indeed, people of color do not merely deserve such reductions; they are widely believed to have a *right* to them. And in this way, environmental justice resembles both mainstream environmentalism and other spheres of contemporary policy advocacy.[10]

The challenges confronting the federal pursuit of environmental justice stem from many factors besides race, some of which will not easily yield to federal policy intervention. These include the sheer density of the policy milieu that environmental justice aspires to influence. A significant historic constraint is simply late arrival at the environmental policy party—well after most of the best seats had already been taken by national environmental groups. These groups had overseen the development of a policymaking regime designed to be immensely permeable to *their* brand of citizen activism.[11] This accounts for some of the mistrust, even hostility, that grassroots activists have often directed toward mainstream environmental organizations.[12] California legal activist Luke Cole captures some of this tension in observing that "the siting of unwanted facilities in neighborhoods where people of color live must not be seen as a *failure* of environmental law, but as a *success* of environmental law. While we may decry the *outcome,* the laws are working as they were designed to work."[13] That is, they were designed to protect the "haves" at the expense of the "have nots."

The bedrock federal statutes of modern environmentalism were enacted between 1969 and 1980; environmental justice activists held their first meetings with EPA administrator William Reilly only in 1990—a full decade after Congress passed the last of these laws, the Comprehensive Environmental Response, Compensation, and Liability Act (CERCLA or "Superfund"). By the time of those meetings the EPA itself was nearly twenty years old and well institutionalized. Many battles had already been fought. Basic structures and procedures were long in place. Part—but only part—of the frustration of environmental justice advocates is attributable to this late start. When environmentalism was coming into its own on the federal agenda, advocates for racial minorities and the poor had other priorities. Even now the political establishment that includes mainstream environmentalism is reluctant to pursue environmental justice through federal statutes, no matter which party controls Congress. Instead, national policy emphasizes the creative use of administrative discretion, an aggressive search for fertile but untilled fields within the existing framework.

Environmental justice must also contend with a decentralized policy process in which business interests hold most of the cards not dealt to establishment environmentalists. And environmental justice must overcome or learn to exploit not only various aspects of federalism (the accumulated weight of powers, policies and private sector activity operating at state and local levels of government) but also the federal-level separation of powers. The EPA functions not only through its national office but also through ten regional offices, each enjoying substantial discretion. Such an overlay of arrangements could not fail to spawn variations in policy approaches across jurisdictions, especially since cities, states, and regions vary widely in the environmental problems they present. One would be mistaken to think that the environmental justice movement wants equity defined as equalized pollution, or as treating "like cases alike." Instead, the movement's overwhelming orientation is both toward an enhanced role for the community and toward various substantive environment-related benefits (including, but by no means limited to, pollution reductions) wherever these seem achievable. Asked, "What do you want?" the improvisational, bottom-up coalition of grassroots organizations and their allies that comprises the environmental justice movement answers: "Whatever we can get, wherever we can get it."

Chapter 2 of this essay reviews some further background essential for understanding how environmental justice advocacy helped generate the current federal initiatives. Chapters 3, 4, and 5 examine central themes of environmental justice advocacy and policy—involvement, health, and opportunity—that are building blocks in the model of policymaking implicitly embraced by environmental justice advocates. This model essentially holds that the disenfranchisement of communities is intimately connected to greater health risks, to unfair environmental burdens, and to diminished opportunities. Ideally, the greater inclusion of communities can help lower risks, reduce burdens, and raise opportunities, thus producing something closer to a just society. Taken together chapters 3, 4, and 5 emphasize: (1) the ideological and practical primacy of community involvement over the other elements of the model, and (2) the variety of limitations and drawbacks that challenge federal efforts on all three fronts.

A concluding chapter suggests the general terms of a reconfigured debate, prodded by institutional arrangements for agenda-setting that would be more likely than conventional environmental justice advocacy to promote healthy and livable minority communities. This alternative approach (envisioned as supplementing, rather than replacing, conventional advocacy) would not emphasize the most vulnerable targets of popular fear and outrage—toxic waste sites, landfills, and so on. Nor would it encourage the boundaryless demands of citizens while avoiding consideration of cost, the confronting of tradeoffs, and the need for a stronger sense of priorities. For these reasons, this orientation is likely to find adherents mostly outside the current environmental justice movement and the policy initiatives inspired by it.

2

FOUNDATIONS

Labels are crucial to mobilizing support for public policy objectives. That is why advocates in fiscal policy debates are inclined to portray tax cuts as "incentives," tax hikes as "revenue enhancements," and spending increases as "investments."[1] Similarly, the terms *environmental justice, equity*, and *racism* reflect a varying set of political imperatives, not neutral descriptive intent or consensus about meaning.[2] Unlike such labels as "segregation" or "environmental protection," the flexible locution "environmental racism" is inherently provocative and was intended to be so. By mobilizing constituencies, casting blame, and generating pressure against targeted institutions, "environmental racism" and "environmental justice" are effective rhetorical tools that have helped pave the way for preferred procedures and policy changes.[3] Academics who write about environmental justice are, as a rule, strikingly unconcerned with the abundant (and ancient) scholarly and philosophical literature addressing equity and justice.[4] The reason appears to be that practical political goals loom far larger than intellectual ones in much of this work.

Environmental equity refers, according to one leading proponent, to "the equal protection of environmental laws."[5] Relatively technical and unprovocative, environmental equity not surprisingly received official sanction during the Bush administration as Environmental Protection Agency (EPA) Administrator William Reilly met with advocates and initiated the first agency assessment of the issue by the EPA's Environmental Equity Workgroup.[6] The EPA defined environmental equity as referring to "the distribution of environmental risks across population groups and to our policy responses to these distributions."[7]

A focus on equity facilitates consideration of the possibility that "a pattern of disparate pollution impact may not arise from overt discrimination in the particular environmental actions examined."[8] Activists have largely eschewed the term, however, out of concern that it may imply a desire merely to redistribute pollution from victimized communities to more fortunate areas. Benjamin F. Chavis Jr., a key movement figure and, briefly, executive director of the National Association for the Advancement of Colored People, was painfully aware of the political and moral pitfalls of such an implication in his address before the First National People of Color Environmental Leadership Summit in October 1991. Professed Chavis: "We are not saying, 'Take the poisons out of our community and put them in a white community.' We are saying that *no* community should have these poisons."[9]

Environmental racism, a more incendiary term, boldly asserts that overt or subtle (often institutional, if unintended) racism underlies variation in the distribution of environmental burdens.[10] Reportedly coined by Chavis, this term simultaneously serves at least three purposes.[11] First, it is provocative and evocative—an excellent media tool. Second, for the same reasons, it is also a superb mobilizing claim, encapsulating the argument that people of color must pay close attention to environmental matters generally and to the specific grievance immediately at issue. Third, the label overtly professes linkage between the previously disparate arenas of environmentalism and civil rights.

In addition, an allegation of environmental racism is meant to place whites, including traditional environmentalists, on the defensive by conjuring anxiety that they may be perceived as racist. As one well-known commentator on racial matters has observed "[racial] vulnerability may cause *more* anxiety in whites who have earnestly worked to put themselves beyond racism, since their investment in racial innocence is greater."[12] Assessing the furor surrounding a proposed oil pipeline in the Los Angeles area, Eugene Grigsby notes that "[m]ere use of the term 'environmental racism' evokes images of conspiratorial abuse. Not surprisingly, elected officials who are inclined to support the pipeline are reluctant to publicly embrace a project tarnished by the charge of racism."[13] In sum, the claim of environmental racism ought to be viewed as just another tool in the considerable repertoire of community advocacy (alongside legal arguments, health anxieties, protest rallies, press releases, and so on).

Environmental justice had, by the beginning of the Clinton presidency, become the favored term among advocates, analysts, policymakers, and the press. Like the movement it describes, the term is all-embracing, virtually a bumper sticker attachable to all manner of procedural and policy vehicles and to all community claims for redress. The term also links, in an upbeat and nontechnical way that environmental equity/racism do not, the major liberal ideals of environmental protection and fairness for disadvantaged persons. The EPA office of environmental justice declares that environmental justice indicates "the fair treatment and meaningful involvement of all people regardless of race, color, national origin, or income with respect to the development, implementation, and enforcement of environmental laws, regulations, and policies."[14] While no one can quarrel with "fairness" or "meaningful involvement" as symbolic language, both are too vague to serve as actual policies, at least as stated by the EPA. At best, the EPA definition is, like the Clinton executive order, an open invitation to debate and to choose policies, not a clear statement of ends agreed to. If "environmental racism" is an exercise in *adversarial* rhetoric, "environmental justice" is quintessentially an *aspirational* term.

Environmental justice activism pursues a wide range of social goals. When the First National People of Color Environmental Leadership Summit convened in Washington, D.C., in October 1991, the seventeen "Principles of Environmental Justice" drafted demanded an end to "the production of all toxins, hazardous wastes and radioactive materials" and to the "testing of experimental reproductive and medical procedures and vaccinations on people of color." The principles affirmed everyone's right to safe and healthy work environments, quality health care, and freedom from the need to choose between unsafe jobs and unemployment. The preamble, modeled on the American Constitution, pronounced the aims of the meeting as including nothing less than "our political, economic and cultural liberation that has been denied for over 500 years of colonization and oppression, resulting in the poisoning of our communities and land and the genocide of our peoples. . . ."[15] Pat Bryant, executive director of the Gulf Coast Tenants Association, a southern advocacy group, offered a similarly broad list of objectives in March 1993 congressional testimony.[16] A primary appeal of the environmental justice rubric clearly lies in the potential leverage it offers regarding objectives that have little immediately to do with pollution. (For the full text of the Principles of Environmental Justice, see Appendix B.)

The summit's principles hint at both the appeal and limitations of environmental justice. Essentially a version of grassroots communitarianism tied to ethnic empowerment yearnings, environmental justice is strong on both outrage and vision. It is also profoundly inclusive, covering racial and class-based inequity, overt and covert practice, programs at every level of government, and, in fact, any imaginable right or slight that any person of color may perceive to be environment-related. In the hands of social justice activists who aspire to an array of goals (such as greater workforce diversity at the EPA, blocking a proposed incinerator, enhanced self-determination for Native American tribes, and so on), environmental justice becomes virtually boundaryless. This is essential to nurturing a diverse movement coalition that might otherwise have little reason to exist. Under the banner of environmental justice any grievance or proposed solution, from any community or grassroots organization, enjoys instant and unquestioned legitimacy. A boundaryless agenda is rooted not only in the raw imperatives of coalition politics but also in a philosophical ideal. Such a movement maximizes prospects for citizen activism and influence and avoids "victimizing" persons or communities whose concerns might otherwise fail to be addressed. This perspective, along with the natural limitations of a fluid social movement, inevitably inhibits potentially disagreeable discussion of priorities and tradeoffs.

Such considerations aside, the political wisdom of a rhetorical shift from "racism" to "justice" is undeniable. In contemporary American political discourse the latter lacks the provocative nuance of the former. Whatever the ultimate ambitions of activists, most persons outside the advocacy community, including especially politicians and officials in government agencies, will be more comfortable with "justice" partly because it connotes a positive goal to be achieved through creative effort, while "racism" highlights blame for failure to achieve it.[17] But vision must come to grips with unpleasant reality. As even most activists will probably admit if pressed, a world in which no person or community faces potential exposure to any environmental toxin is an impossible dream.

Origins

The face of mainstream environmentalism throughout its rise to prominence in the 1960s, 1970s, and at least through the mid-1980s was overwhelmingly white and middle-class. This was also true of its predecessor, the conservation movement that worked successfully over the years for such public amenities as protected wilderness and a national park system.[18] Not surprisingly the agendas of racial minorities and low-income citizens, and of politicians and organizations claiming to speak on behalf of these specific needs, made little room for the "hiking and biking" brand of environmentalism.[19]

African Americans simply had more pressing business: securing basic rights of access to crucial institutions and winning policies designed to mitigate an array of social, economic, and political disadvantages.

Moreover, the purposive incentives that motivated organizational participation among middle- and upper-middle-class whites in traditional environmentalism proved, predictably enough, largely incapable of doing so among blacks and low-income persons.[20] This limitation and the political potency of the rhetoric of racism noted earlier are essential to bear in mind when considering the frequent claim that the paucity of minority faces among mainstream environmental groups reflects "institutional racism."

In fact, nothing so sinister is necessary to account for the limited appeal of traditional environmentalism among minorities. Lack of minority participation in such groups, especially before about 1980, resulted from a natural mismatch between the incentive structures of these groups and what would have been necessary to motivate significant minority membership. Generally speaking, few voluntary associations are supermarkets; most are specialty boutiques with one goal, or perhaps a few related and easily compatible ones. Persons to whom the goal does not strongly appeal do not join the organization. This goals-and-incentives choice, usually made at an organization's founding and confirmed by organizational survival, is virtually inevitable (although not entirely unalterable). Viewed in this light, accusing a largely liberal national environmental group of institutional racism is akin to blaming the NAACP for failing to highlight Native American or feminist concerns that it was not created to address in the first place.[21]

With prominent African Americans sometimes excoriating environmentalism as a damaging national distraction from the more pressing challenges of uplifting the poor and saving the cities, it is not surprising that racial minorities were scarce among the leaderships and memberships of major environmental organizations. Minority politicians, including members of Congress, provided dependable votes for environmental legislation but relatively little environmental policy leadership.[22] Whitney M. Young Jr., head of the National Urban League in the years immediately prior to his death in 1971, declared: "The war on pollution is one that should be waged after the war on poverty is won. Common sense calls for reasonable national priorities and not for inventing new causes whose main appeal seems to be in their potential for copping out and ignoring the most dangerous and pressing of our problems."[23] Richard Hatcher, the nationally visible black mayor of Gary, Indiana, offered a similar sentiment in an August 1970 *Time* magazine article on "The Rise of Anti-Ecology." Hatcher bitingly complained that "the nation's concern with the environment has done what George Wallace was unable to do: distract the nation from the human problems of Black and Brown Americans."[24]

A considerable amount of today's environmental justice advocacy would probably have made sense to both Young and Hatcher. For one thing, in today's environmental justice movement, people of color are not merely prominent but dominant. Just as significant, the movement professes a broader vision of environmentalism that highlights the vulnerability of poor and nonwhite persons to industrial pollution and to the perceived predations of corporate capital. In fact, Mayor Hatcher himself clearly moved toward just such a vision in Gary, Indiana, long before it had a name.[25] Still, it is important to grasp the relative indifference or hostility of African Americans toward traditional environmentalism during this period to understand why the issue of racial equity, much in evidence later, was little discussed. This in turn meant that while the bedrock environmental legislation of the late 1960s and 1970s—the National Environmental Policy Act of 1969, the Clean Air Act Amendments of 1970, the Federal Water Pollution Control Act of 1972, and others— was being enacted, little thought was given to how minority and low-income communities would fare at the hands of either business or government regulators.

What changed to produce a national "people of color" brand of environmentalism? Ironically, such a movement may have become possible only because of the rise of a particular kind of environmental anxiety in the population at-large. The watershed episode was the prolonged political crisis in the Love Canal neighborhood of

Niagara Falls, New York. The now-legendary events are summarized by Mark E. Rushefsky:

> Niagara [Falls] is the location of the infamous Love Canal, formerly a toxic waste dump that leaked into the surrounding neighborhood, including the school built on the site. [Neighborhood resident Lois] Gibbs, concerned about the hazard and lack of response by local and state officials, began a door-to-door survey of her neighbors to discover the extent of harm and to mobilize the community. A Love Canal Homeowners Association was formed, with Gibbs as its head, that pressured local, state and federal officials to take action. Eventually, the state bought the inner ring of homes near the dump and took action to prevent further leakage. The Love Canal incident was instrumental in the passage of the Comprehensive Environmental Response, Compensation, and Liability Act, better known as Superfund, in 1980.[26]

Considerable subsequent analysis has suggested that the hysteria at Love Canal was very likely disproportionate to the actual health threat neighborhood residents faced.[27] In political terms, however, the crises in Love Canal and other communities (in tandem with a 1982 public uproar over Reagan administration mismanagement of the hazardous waste program) were incontestably powerful.[28] The wave of attention and anxiety Love Canal generated not only propelled the enactment of ambitious and costly hazardous waste cleanup legislation but also produced a vastly heightened public awareness and fear of dumps and toxic sites generally.[29]

One significant result was the rise of a kind of grassroots mobilization quite unlike traditional environmentalism. Localistic, public health-oriented, participatory and often poorly funded (unlike its national, ecology-minded, bureaucratized, staff-directed, and more affluent counterpart), this new type of organization has been a conspicuous feature of the post-1980 policy landscape.[30] A particularly effective spur to the creation of a grassroots environmental group is any effort to site a "locally unwanted land use" (LULU) in a community. Proposed incinerators, landfills and treatment plants often incite intense local opposition that quickly leads the most energetic, resourceful and articulate opponents into assuming roles as organizational entrepreneurs. It is no coincidence that the so-called NIMBY (not in my back yard) phenomenon took hold as Love Canal and other episodes of local "toxic terror" mobilized mass awareness of sites and facilities about which communities had once been relatively passive.

It is also not surprising that this phenomenon should have arisen in racially charged form within minority communities. African Americans, in particular, have historically confronted persistent discrimination, spatial concentration, and lagging incomes, yielding a group identity powerfully anchored in perceptions of long-term collective disadvantage.[31] Once a heightened general awareness and fear of facilities that treat, store or dispose of toxic material had taken hold in mass opinion, it would not take long for communities (and especially persons with activist inclinations) to link an enduring sense of victimization (augmented by the well-honed tools of protest politics) to this newly salient threat, especially since many African Americans live in industrial areas. As Robert D. Bullard puts it, toxic threats meant that environmentalism could be "couched in a civil rights context beginning in the early 1980s."[32] Moreover, environmental justice would adopt a key strategic posture of the civil rights movement: expansion of the scope of local conflict onto the national stage in the hope that federal authorities would help provide leverage over state and local ones.

Allegations that the black community was bearing an unfair share of society's LULU burden had begun surfacing even before Love Canal made headlines. In Houston a 1979 civil rights case brought on behalf of a mostly African American neighborhood challenged the siting of a dump. Although the plaintiffs did not prevail in *Bean v. Southwestern Waste Management Corporation* that case is widely regarded as "the parent of environmental justice litigation."[33]

The landmark community mobilization against a pending siting occurred in Warren County, North Carolina in 1982.[34] Bullard observes that it was "the first national protest by blacks on the hazardous waste issue."[35] Indeed, it is difficult to imagine a largely

African American community mounting so militant or so resonant a protest a decade earlier.

After the cleanup of contaminated waste oil illegally dumped along more than 200 miles of North Carolina roadway, the soil remained contaminated with polychlorinated biphenyls (PCBs). The state's decision to bury this soil in a landfill site in the town of Afton sparked community mobilization and the formation of the Warren County Citizens Concerned About PCBs. Organizers received the support of Charles E. Cobb, former executive director of the United Church of Christ's Commission for Racial Justice, who decried the siting as emblematic of widespread official disregard for the environmental health of poor and black communities. The resulting protests and mass arrests drew the direct participation of the leadership of both the commission and the Southern Christian Leadership Conference, as well as District of Columbia congressional delegate Walter E. Fauntroy.

The trucks ultimately rolled and the landfill opened despite the protest. But the intense community resistance compelled Democratic governor James B. Hunt to offer concessions, including the promise, according to one account, that "no more landfills would be built in Warren County and that well water and body levels would be monitored."[36] Activists point to the Warren County protest as having demonstrated the potential for a new vision of environmental activism. In fundamental respects what had been discovered was simply the possibility for an effectively racialized NIMBY advocacy.

Evidence

Delegate Fauntroy requested the legislative branch's investigative and auditing agency, the General Accounting Office (GAO), to examine the relationship between the location of hazardous waste landfills and the racial and economic status of the surrounding communities.[37] The resulting 1983 report addressed "off-site" landfills— that is, "those not part of or contiguous to an industrial facility"—in EPA's Deep South Region 4.[38] The report identified four such landfills among the region's eight states. Three of the four were located in "areas"—that is, "subdivisions of political jurisdictions designated by the census for data gathering"—with majority black populations. In descending order, these areas held black population percentages of 90, 66, 52 and 38. (The Warren County landfill lay in the 66 percent black area.) The percentage of population below the poverty level in these areas ranged between 42 and 26 percent, with virtually all the poor being African American.

Although environmental justice advocates emphasize the GAO finding that three of four sites resided in predominantly black areas, the conclusions that can be drawn from this and similar work are limited. One reason is that the kinds of "area" serving as the unit of analysis in such research are often so large that they may disguise considerable heterogeneity; a facility located in a largely white subarea may nevertheless be interpreted as "minority" because the larger area it embraces contains many such persons.[39] It should be noted that a large number of whites and nonpoor persons resided in relative proximity to these sites. This is not therefore (although it theoretically could be) racial discrimination in the classic sense: second-class treatment directed only at individuals of a particular racial group.

A study of "off-site" landfills can reveal little about the overall distribution of the waste stream, because off-site facilities take in only a minuscule portion of America's waste. Furthermore, the current demographic pattern in a given area may be misleading; the local ethnic mix at the time a facility was constructed may have differed considerably, undermining the argument that racism underlay the original siting decision.[40] James T. Hamilton notes this complicating possibility in the following terms:

> A facility may locate in a given area, causing the environment to deteriorate and housing prices to drop. Residents who place a high value on the environment may vote with their feet and leave the community. The residents that remain or move in may be low-income, minority residents who lack the resources to purchase a higher level of environmental amenities. This potential for neighborhoods to

change as they become polluted means that studies based on the current exposure of different demographic groups to pollution provide
evidence on disparate impact but not necessarily on discriminatory
intent since one may need information on the neighborhoods when
facilities were sited to analyze causation.[41]

Another important limitation is that such a study can reveal
nothing about the ways or extent to which facilities might pose a
hazard to human health. One learns nothing about chemical exposures—although advocates sometimes employ "exposure" or
"burden" as a catch-all synonym for both proximity and more
direct contact—or about the extent to which human health might
be put at risk. Evidence and technical analysis relating to risk or
health impacts tend to play only a small role in the anxiety and
advocacy directed at such facilities. Indeed, environmental justice
supporters are often suspicious of, and even openly hostile to, risk
assessments that endeavor to address such impacts.[42]

Similar limitations apply to a far more elaborate report on race-
based environmental unfairness. In 1987, four years after the GAO
study, the Commission for Racial Justice released *Toxic Wastes and
Race in the United States*.[43] The report presented two different analyses of demographic patterns. The unit of analysis was residential
zip codes rather than census areas. The first analysis examines
commercial hazardous waste facilities, which are defined as any
public or private facility "which accepts hazardous wastes from a
third party for a fee or other remuneration."[44] The study found race
to be "the most significant among variables tested in association
with the location of commercial hazardous waste facilities,"
observing that,

> Communities with the greatest number of commercial hazardous
> waste facilities had the highest composition of racial and ethnic res-
> idents. In communities with two or more facilities or one of the
> nation's five largest landfills, the average minority percentage of the
> population was more than three times that of communities without
> facilities (38 percent versus 12 percent).[45]

A second "descriptive" part of the report examined "uncontrolled toxic waste sites," reaching similar conclusions. It found that "more than half of the population in the United States lived in residential ZIP code areas with one or more uncontrolled toxic waste sites." The study also found that three of every five black and Hispanic Americans lived in such communities.[46] The data base included 18,164 sites then in EPA's Comprehensive Environmental Response, Compensation, and Liability Act Information System (CERCLIS).

Like the GAO study, the more elaborate analysis in *Toxic Wastes and Race in the United States* could not assess the risk associated with alleged siting disparities. There is no way of knowing what these sites expose the relevant communities to (if anything), at what levels, how likely exposure might be (if it not currently occurring), or what the health effects of such exposure would be, assuming there would be any effects at all. For many traditional environmentalists and environmental justice advocates alike, such uncertainty is precisely the point. Since no one can precisely surmise how dangerous any given chemical potpourri is or might be—and since risk assessment pretends to a value neutrality it cannot actually achieve—is it not far better to clean up (and prevent) as many of them as possible on the reasonable grounds that precautionary action is at the worst not harmful, while inaction may cost health and perhaps even lives?

Exposure and risk aside, *Toxic Wastes and Race in the United States* fails as a persuasive analysis for at least three reasons. One problem is simple data quality. In building a data set, many sites are hard to label accurately for locational purposes since inadequate information is available. As Kelley A. Crews-Meyer and Wayne R. Meyer point out, for hazardous waste facilities "there is the additional potential danger that any address given may be an office address instead of the site address, as many times offices are located off-site."[47] Second, as noted above, off-site commercial hazardous waste facilities handle only a fraction of all hazardous waste—an estimated 3 or 4 percent; the remainder is processed on-site by the entity that generates it.[48] Thus, while the study might lead one to suspect inequity in the overall distribution of hazardous waste—indeed one should be surprised if variation in its distribution were not the norm—the report offers no reliable assessment of this. Third, the commission finding that communities with either multiple facilities or the largest landfills are on average 38 percent minority, also means that such areas remain, on average, more than 60 percent nonminority. Such a finding, however compelling to environmental justice enthusiasts, potentially complicates the political and policy task facing anyone wishing to design and promote policies aimed at alleviating the burden on minorities. If environmental racism exists, its effects must spill over onto whites, perhaps in some cases onto far more whites than minorities.

Although the GAO and United Church of Christ studies have probably been the most widely cited examinations of geographical disparities, there have been many others. Hamilton found that commercial hazardous waste facilities targeted for capacity expansion had an average nonwhite population of 25 percent versus 18 percent for areas without expansion. He suggested that differences in the probability that residents would mobilize in effective opposition (as indicated by percentage of residents registered to vote) best explained which neighborhoods were targeted.[49] Paul Mohai and Bunyan Bryant, using a sample of Detroit area residents, found that within 1 mile of commercial hazardous waste facilities, the population was 48 percent minority and 29 percent poor; this decreased to 39 percent and 18 percent at a distance of 1 to 1.5 miles, and to 18 percent and 10 percent beyond 1.5 miles.[50] As far back as the 1970s, well before the advent of any focused advocacy regarding such disparities, studies suggested that minorities and low-income persons living in urban areas faced significantly higher air pollution exposures.[51]

Law professor Vicki Been has argued that efforts to address any racial disparity in facility siting must come to grips with the historical question of which came first at a given location, the facility or the minority community? If persons of low income and noxious facilities are both economically drawn to the same cheap land, it is possible that a black neighborhood might spring up or expand near such a facility. As Been writes:

> If the neighborhoods were disproportionately populated by people of color or the poor at the time the siting decisions were made, a reasonable inference can be drawn that the siting process had a disproportionate effect upon the poor and people of color. In that case, changes in the siting process may be required.
>
> On the other hand, if, after the LULU was built, the neighborhoods in which LULUs were sited became increasingly poor, or became home to an increasing percentage of people of color, the cure for the problem of disproportionate siting is likely to be much more complicated and difficult.[52]

Allegations of racially biased environmental enforcement have also sparked concern. Advocates rely especially on an often-cited 1992 study by Marianne Lavelle and Marcia Coyle published by the *National Law Journal*.[53] The report alleges two sorts of bias. One claim is that hazardous waste sites in areas with the lowest minority populations made it to the Superfund's National Priorities List (NPL) faster, on average, than sites in areas having larger minority populations. Average waiting time among sites in the 290 "whitest" areas—that is, areas were the population was more than 98.3 percent white—was 4.69 years. But among the 290 sites in areas that were at least 15.9 percent minority, waiting time to reach NPL status was 5.63 years—a difference of almost one year.

Furthermore, the report calculates that penalties imposed in court for violations of the Resource Conservation and Recovery Act (RCRA) "at sites having the greatest white population were about 500 percent higher than penalties at sites with the greatest minority population." In dollar terms, cases in "white areas" averaged $335,566, while fines levied in cases filed in "minority areas" averaged only $55,318. Average penalties imposed in court for *all* violations of environmental laws showed white areas again leading. Fines in white areas averaged $153,067, while the figure for minority areas was \$105,028. Moreover, at least in certain of EPA's regions, the pace of cleanup is far slower for minority communities.[54]

How "significant" are these findings? The findings had clear *political* significance as they offered environmental justice advocates welcome and timely quantitative support for their claim of profoundly unequal treatment. As is clear from the text of the report, EPA officials were critical of its methodology but also plainly defensive. The EPA suggested, in essence, that the variation displayed may be attributable to many factors (including, for example, differences between urban versus rural areas; a handful of large awards in a few cases; or some unperceived "technical" factor that happens to correlate, or to appear to correlate, with race or income). The study does not attempt either to test for, or to correct for, the possible influence of such factors. This study leaves a reader to wonder about the *statistical* significance of its results (that is, the likelihood that any of its various findings might have been obtained by chance) since the authors conducted no tests to gauge such significance.

Much of the seminal environmental justice research (especially those efforts bearing an advocacy tone) has been called into serious question either on methodological grounds or by noncorroborative results. A statistical consultant retained by the EPA to assess the *National Law Journal* findings identified "serious statistical methodological problems severely limiting the value of any of the statistical comparisons presented."[55] Bernard Siskin found that differences in average penalties for RCRA violations and for the stringency of Superfund cleanup decisions (treatment versus containment) were not statistically significant, and that racial differences in the speed at which sites were placed on the Superfund National Priorities List appeared significant only because the study failed to account for the correct date on which sites were first discovered.

The *National Law Journal* finding of bias in the penalty structure of Superfund enforcement has been rigorously challenged by Mark Atlas for a number of glaring errors, especially "its failure to control for the effects upon penalties of variables other than areas' race and income characteristics."[56] Atlas's original research argues that "the nature of the case"—the law violated, the nature of its resolution, whether the case involves one or multiple facilities, whether the case is brought against a public or private facility—tends to explain the penalty imposed. Atlas concluded that "there is no evidence that facilities that violate environmental laws in areas that are disproportionately minority or low income tend to be penalized less than other facilities. None of [Atlas's] analyses demonstrated any meaningful relationship between income characteristics and penalties."[57] Ironically, race achieved only a modest relationship with penalties, but in the *opposite* direction than might be thought—facilities in minority areas received *higher* penalties than those in nonminority areas.

Researchers at the Social and Demographic Research Institute (SADRI) at the University of Massachusetts (Amherst) found that analysis using census tracts, rather than the much larger and generally less homogeneous zip codes employed in *Toxic Wastes and Race in the United States,* yielded "no consistent and statistically significant differences in the racial or ethnic composition of tracts that contain commercial TSDFs [treatment storage and disposal facilities] and those that do not."[58]

John A. Hird found that counties that were more than about 12 percent minority (that is, counties with minority percentages greater than the national average) tended to have more sites on the Superfund's National Priorities List than others. But he also found that wealthier counties also had more sites and that when a sub-county comparison was attempted, the relationship with race disappeared. Perhaps most strikingly, the areas surrounding the "worst" sites (that is, the 35 sites scoring above 60 on the Superfund Hazard Ranking System) tended to have "lower poverty rates, lower unemployment rates, lower percentages of nonwhites, and higher median housing values, all in contrast to allegations that these sites disproportionately affect the poor and minorities."[59] It is important to remember, however, that any analysis based on a system of formally designated sites is inherently suspect as an indicator of the actual "distribution of pollution." At its inception Superfund's Hazard Ranking System included, in effect, a "political variable" designed to distribute program resources relatively widely.[60]

In a recent paper for a committee on environmental justice sponsored by the Institute of Medicine, Brett Baden and Don Coursey found race to be relatively unimportant historically in the placement of waste sites in the city of Chicago. Instead, they conclude that

> past waste-generating activities tended to be in less populous, lower income areas with good access to highways and waterways. Present waste sites tend to be located in less populous, more wealthy neighborhoods, with convenient access to transportation infrastructure. There is no good evidence that African Americans of any income class are more likely to live in areas with more concentrated waste sites in the city of Chicago, or that they have been targeted to be disproportionately exposed to the most hazardous waste.[61]

The General Accounting Office, which provided welcome ammunition for the emerging environmental justice movement in its much-heralded 1983 report on four southern sites, comes to a different conclusion in a much more elaborate 1995 survey of nonhazardous municipal landfills: "We found that the percentage of minorities and low-income people living within one mile of nonhazardous municipal landfills was more often lower than the percentage in the rest of the county. When the data from our sample were used to make estimates about all nonhazardous municipal landfills in the nation, neither minorities nor low-income people were overrepresented near landfills in any consistent manner."[62]

Ann O'M. Bowman and Kelley A. Crews-Meyer examined facilities that generate hazardous waste along with those that treat, store, or dispose of it within counties in EPA's Region 4, the area covered by the 1983 GAO study.[63] They find that "race and class have a conditional relationship with regard to hazardous waste activity" meaning that "in counties with relatively low income levels, percent black has one effect while in areas of relatively high income, percent black has a different effect."[64] But race and class together explain only about one-third of the variance. Population size turns out to be more strongly associated with hazardous waste activity. Conclude Bowman and Crews-Meyer: "Because larger counties in this region, on average, tend to have lower proportions of African Americans and higher levels of income, statistical analysis produces findings that dispute the environmental equity thesis."[65]

Christopher Boerner and Thomas Lambert have observed that many studies suffer from severe methodological difficulties or are too limited in scope to reliably indicate broader patterns.[66] Indeed, once contrary findings and thoughtful criticisms are taken adequately into account, even a reasonably generous reading of the foundational empirical research alleging environmental inequity along racial lines must leave room for profound skepticism regarding the reported results. Taken as a whole this research offers, at best, only tenuous support for the hypothesis of racial inequity in siting or exposure, and no insight into the crucial issues of risk and health impact.

Beyond Evidence

Even if the existing evidence were more uniformly supportive of the view that measurable environmental injustice is pervasive, important unanswered questions remain. Metaphorically speaking, even if one assumes that the existence of so much smoke must indicate a fire somewhere, which fires does one fight first or hardest? With what equipment does one fight them? Conspicuous fires may be gratifying to fight but might doing so leave smoldering embers that pose greater long-term damage? Is fighting every fire equally hard at every location a sensible path to equity? Studies such as those reported above, whether supportive of environmental justice claims or not, offer little guidance on reasonable policy priorities and approaches.

A second and deeper problem, however, is that formal analysis is to a considerable extent irrelevant to the underlying objectives and gratifications that stir activist and community enthusiasm for environmental justice. Although sympathetic accounts of the movement's rise generally highlight the GAO and United Church of Christ/Commission for Racial Justice studies, these crude assessments were always merely instruments of the movement rather than its cause. Although further and more refined analyses will always be helpful, it would be naive to imagine that their conclusions (whatever they might be) will matter much to communities unless somehow bonded to a gratifying practical politics anchored within those communities.

The environmental justice perspective is powerfully ascendant not because it speaks honestly to technical questions of harm or risk—it often does not do this—but because it promises something larger, more uplifting, and more viscerally engaging than mere careful calculation can approach. It effectively speaks to the fear and anger among local communities feeling overwhelmed by forces beyond their control and outraged by what they perceive to be assaults on their collective quality of life. Vicki Been suggests that to some extent "the quest for justice in the siting of LULUs is the flipside of the inequitable municipal services movement of the 1960s, [which] charged that communities disproportionately placed 'goods' such as street lamps, libraries, and other beneficial services in wealthy neighborhoods to the exclusion of poor neighborhoods."[67]

One potential source of confusion for anyone trying to think carefully about this subject is that, although environmental justice often deploys technical language and cites formal analyses when useful, this activity is at root political, not technical. The movement's use of technical language stems largely from its often awkward, improvisational, and intuitive groping for response from an establishment believed: (a) to require such language as the price of admission to the policy process or (b) to deploy technical expertise as a weapon of either oppression or self-defense. Although activists make regular—sometimes almost mantra-like—reference to the environmental bureaucracy's paltry capacity for addressing "multiple, cumulative, and synergistic risks," such language does not mean that activists are committed to a technical perspective.

Quite the opposite is the case. Like grassroots advocacy generally, environmental justice reflects a challenge to technocracy, and to technical ways of thinking, not an embrace of them.[68] Benjamin Chavis quite clearly saw the Commission for Racial Justice report in this light, as a useful "departure from our traditional protest methodology" rather than as symptomatic of a new devotion to a scientific view of health and risk. Activists and angry community residents are disinclined to allow epidemiologists, toxicologists, and statisticians to define the premises of their movement. Moreover, race and social justice concerns aside, there also exists a well-documented disjunction between expert and citizen perspectives on risk.[69] Visible and involuntary risks have a much greater intuitive lock on the perceptions of ordinary citizens than they do on risk management professionals. Not surprisingly then, critiques of the quantitative literature by earnest academics and policy researchers do not resonate within the movement or within communities. And in the long run, this divergence in perspective is perhaps the most fundamental challenge environmental justice policymaking faces.

Initiatives: Groping for Justice

As the 1990s dawned, advocacy by scholars and activists generated attention among federal policymakers. A January 1990 University of Michigan Conference on Race and the Incidence of Environmental Hazards led to meetings with EPA Administrator William Reilly and, in turn, to his decision to create an Environmental Equity Workgroup charged with reviewing the problem.[70] In 1992 the EPA, the Agency for Toxic Substances and Disease Registry (ATSDR), and the National Institute for Environmental Health Sciences (NIEHS) jointly sponsored a workshop addressing environmental equity.[71]

By 1992 the issue had found at least fragmentary congressional sponsorship. Representative John Lewis (D-Georgia) and Senator Al Gore (D-Tennessee) introduced a proposed Environmental Justice Act. This legislation would have required the EPA to identify the 100 counties or other geographical units in the United States containing the highest total weight of toxic chemicals, areas to be classified as Environmental High Impact Areas. This designation would trigger both regular facility inspections by the EPA and the Occupational Safety and Health Administration, as well as health impact assessments to determine "the nature and extent, if any, of acute and chronic impacts on human health." A permitting and siting moratorium would ensue in areas of significant adverse health impacts.[72] Representative Cardiss Collins (D-Illinois) sponsored an Environmental Equal Rights Act to allow citizen petitions to prevent the siting of waste facilities in "environmentally disadvantaged" communities.[73]

Neither bill came close to passage. As with many legislative proposals, raising the profile of the issue, rather than enacting new legislation, may have been the real motive behind their introduction. By late 1994 already dim prospects for any significant congressional action on environmental justice would be snuffed out entirely by the election of a far more conservative Republican Congress. The Republican agenda for regulatory reform would challenge even relatively well established aspects of federal environmental policy. More specifically, the conservative lexicon has tended to define environmental injustice as excessive regulatory encroachment on private property rights, something entirely different from what environmental justice activists and their allies had in mind.[74]

However, the 1992 election of the first Democratic administration since the enactment of Superfund (in the waning days of the lame-duck Carter presidency) and the presence of environmental justice advocates Chavis and Bullard on the Clinton transition team provided conditions favorable to presidential consideration of the issue. Advocates supplied ideas for institutionalizing environmental justice that the incoming administration would reflect.

Deeohn Ferris, an African American attorney who had spent several years at the EPA before becoming program director of the environmental justice project at the Lawyers' Committee for Civil Rights Under Law, spearheaded a coalition of activist organizations, the Environmental Justice Transition Group, which submitted detailed recommendations to the transition team.[75] One idea that bore fruit quickly was consolidation of the EPA's Indian program activities into a single office. A far more ambitious recommendation called on the new president to issue an executive order "providing for the equitable implementation of environmental programs."[76] The group urged that the executive order establish a "Federal Coordinating Council on environmental justice" comprised of agencies and departments to: (1) "review federal research and research systems, report on gaps and other deficiencies in environmental data, research priorities and compatibility of federal research systems" and (2) "institute a framework for technology assessment and examine related issues in the context of social, cultural and political impact."[77] The coalition was calling for a wide-ranging, open-ended, federally sponsored inquiry that would deepen and refine the critique of environmental and social policy to which the coalition subscribed. The results of this research effort could conceivably have facilitated the setting of environmental justice priorities. But the coalition's insistence on such a broad-gauged contextual framework suggests that such priorities would actually be maddeningly hard to arrive at. The coalition aimed not at priority-setting but at winning mechanisms that would offer members, and the larger movement on whose behalf the coalition spoke, maximum representative and procedural leverage.

Aware of the powerful procedural weapon that the National Environmental Policy Act's environmental impact statement process had provided to opponents of many federally funded activities, the coalition suggested an environmental justice analogue: the "equity impact statement." Such statements should, said the coalition, "be required for all major federal regulations, grants, and projects" and incorporate "a presumption equally protecting all people from pollution."[78]

While the administration did not implement this recommendation, the new EPA administrator, Carol Browner, quickly embraced another: creation of a federal advisory body, chartered under the Federal Advisory Committee Act. An idea supported by Ferris but regarded skeptically by many other activists, the advisory committee was to counsel both the EPA and the Federal Coordinating Council and would "include indigenous peoples and representatives of community based groups experiencing disproportionate impact; and direct federal agencies to develop and institute environmentally beneficial procurement practices emphasizing pollution prevention and environmentally friendly products."[79] As will be shown in the next chapter, the environmental justice community got much the kind of council it wanted soon after Clinton's inauguration.

Not surprisingly, a presidential executive order on environmental justice would take somewhat longer since it would apply to multiple federal agencies and departments and perhaps also to state and local programs interacting with them. A late revision in the text of executive order 12898, which Clinton issued in February 1994 instructing federal agencies to integrate environmental justice into their ongoing missions, was the deletion of a provision requiring "non-federal agencies or entities . . . to submit assurances and compliance reports demonstrating observance of the principles" in the order.[80] This provision would have given the executive order greater reach into the levels of government where most environmentally sensitive siting decisions are made. According to one knowledgeable EPA official, the provision did not survive state protests that it amounted to an unfunded mandate.

Nevertheless, as finally released by the administration, the executive order provided much for activists to cheer. A president had accorded environmental injustice recognition as a "problem" and proposed something that at least smacked of a coordinated response. The "Federal Coordinating Council" called for in Deeohn Ferris's transition memo emerged in the order as an "interagency Federal Working Group on Environmental Justice" comprised of representatives from 17 executive branch entities, ranging from the EPA and the Department of Health and Human Services to the Department of Defense and the White House Office of Science and Technology Policy. Most significantly, the order insisted that:

> To the greatest extent practicable and permitted by law, and consistent with the principles set forth in the report on the National Performance Review, each Federal agency shall make achieving environmental justice part of its mission by identifying and addressing, as appropriate, disproportionately high and adverse human health or environmental effects of its programs, policies and activities on minority populations and low income populations. . . .[81]

In dramatic and predictable contrast to the all-embracing Principles of Environmental Justice, the executive order emphasizes three policy instruments: participation, data collection, and agency procedural milestones. Under the terms of the order the federal government would be attentive to the new grassroots voices, pursue and evaluate new information, and hold itself to procedural implementation timetables. Agencies would have to produce formal environmental justice strategy documents stipulating how they proposed to incorporate the order. As will be argued in subsequent chapters, however, although giving voice to previously silent or underrepresented communities has been both the movement's central demand and government's primary institutional response, this democratizing effort remains deeply problematic, quite apart from the questionable empirical evidence that has helped propel it.

3

INVOLVEMENT

THERE EXISTS no clear and universally accepted definition of environmental justice, but some notion of effective citizen participation and empowerment underlies everyone's conception of it. A fairly typical statement can be found in *Furthering the Principles of Environmental Justice*, a paper produced for a 1995 Princeton University conference on environmental justice, which describes the concept as:

> the main impetus for institutionalized racism and discrimination is the lack of representation and political power of minority groups. Minority groups need to be better incorporated into the decision-making process. The existing imbalances in representation tends [sic] to dictate the future of certain groups. This practice needs to be corrected through the actual empowerment of communities.[1]

Normative belief in citizens and communities having a more significant voice in everything from scientific assessment to facility permitting lies at the core of environmental justice (and grassroots environmentalism generally), both as activism and as federal policy. This focus on democratic principle has antecedents in the Great Society's thrust for "maximum feasible participation" by the poor in the community action programs of the 1960s and also in the New Public Administration that emerged shortly thereafter.[2] But while the environmental justice literature's allegations of racism and disproportionate environmental burdens have been crucial to placing the issue on the federal policy agenda, both our collective experience with public participation and the nature of environmental policy mechanisms suggest significant barriers to effective redress. Perhaps the most serious limitation of community involvement efforts is that they are almost entirely consultative, not authoritative, in nature. To date, the Clinton administration's main environmental justice message has not been "govern thyself!" Rather, it has been something more like "advise us, and we'll get back to you."[3]

One of the six sections of executive order 12898, which Bill Clinton issued in February 1994 to mandate the integration of environmental justice into federal policy, specifically addresses "public participation and access to information."[4] The accompanying presidential memorandum on environmental justice stresses that the executive order intends, among other things "to provide minority communities and low-income communities access to public information on, and an opportunity for public participation in, matters relating to human health or the environment."[5] The memorandum insists that all federal agencies "shall provide opportunities for community input in the NEPA [National Environmental Policy Act] process, including identifying potential effects and mitigation measures in consultation with affected communities and improving the accessibility of meetings, crucial documents, and notices."[6] When President Clinton signed the executive order, EPA administrator Carol Browner promised:

> We will develop strategies to bring justice to Americans who are suffering disproportionately. . . . We will develop strategies to ensure that low-income and minority communities have access to information about their environment—and that they have an opportunity to participate in shaping the government policies that affect their health and environment.[7]

Proponents of participation harbor various objectives. Business firms covet good public relations and new investment opportunities. Government officials are anxious to make programs both more accessible and less threatening. As noted earlier, activists are committed to various ends (such as stopping a proposed incinerator or enhancing tribal self-determination). These varied motivations stem from what James A. Morone characterizes as a deeply American "democratic wish" transcending race and class. It is an aspiration for "the direct participation of a united people pursuing a shared communal interest."[8] Pursuit of environmental justice is a potentially daunting and confusing enterprise largely because of the mix of motives and strategies, embracing both high moral and pragmatic "street-level" goals.

Passion and Compassion

Powerful but diffuse local passions are both a crucial resource and a critical challenge for the environmental justice movement. The emotion-packed comments that follow were delivered at the January 1995 session of the National Environmental Justice Advisory Council (NEJAC).[9] They are reproduced at length for two reasons. First, it is important to comprehend the raw emotion associated with environmental justice. Second, these comments also vividly illustrate the wide range of themes (wellness, fairness, community empowerment, solidarity, diversity, impatience with technical expertise, prosperity, quality of life, and so on) that citizens are inclined to raise under the rubric of environmental justice. Such a range of aspirations would challenge even a resourceful and fully committed government effort founded on strong legislation and bipartisan support, advantages that environmental justice so far lacks.

> The EPA Region 3 recently conducted an environmental exposure assessment of numerous pollutant impacts on Chester [Pennsylvania] and found significant health threats in the midst of our deplorable living conditions. EPA has documented risks 2.5 times

greater than average of cancer and noncancer health effects due to air pollution. An alarming widespread elevated blood lead level in our children is robbing them of their future. . . . I did not come here to tell you about the scientific data. I didn't come here to tell you about causation or risk assessment, factors, and so forth. I have neither a PhD nor MD. However, I can tell you about suffering. I can tell you that we are suffering. We have become experts in suffering, while the EPA, the [state environmental officials] and the federal government are conducting meetings. I came to express to you the intended exploitation of my community. I came to tell you of the comforts that other people gain through our suffering. I came to tell you that the residents of Chester are being trampled on, both civic and basic human rights are being denied. I want to tell you that the future of our children continues to be bargained away by political favors and the color of money. I can tell you about our children who have to dart through the streets to avoid 800 trucks per day. I can tell you about allergies and asthma, and respiratory problems that our people are experiencing. I can tell you about the tornadoes of dust and dirt that blow as if we were in Kansas. I can tell you about the smells that emerge from these facilities that invade our lives like incoming shells, like bombs, bombing someone's house. Smells of burning sewage, chlorine, trash, rotten eggs, and burning flesh. I can tell you of the men who earn $7.16 an hour who are being stuck by dirty needles while working at an autoclave facility. I can tell you these things because I'm an expert on that. . . . (Zulene Mayfield, resident of Chester, Pennsylvania)

West Ambler is a small community located in central Montgomery County [Pennsylvania], about 15 miles north of Philadelphia. . . . Because Ambler is such a small community, the residents are like a family and we are really close-knit. . . . Me, my family, and other residents in my neighborhood are being murdered. We are being poisoned by asbestos. And what's worse is the fact that we are knowingly being poisoned by asbestos.

Asbestos is listed as a carcinogen by the EPA. Any dosage is considered unsafe. Exposure can cause cancer, and other lung diseases. . . . Ambler is a small town, divided along racial lines with one section being comprised of 90 percent African-Americans. This African-American section is home to abandoned asbestos landfills. . . .

. . . No effort was made to prevent access to the dumpsite and the children routinely played on it. . . . We know, of course, that there is no more favorite play area than the one for which adults have excluded by fence or other means. They told me stories of making caves, fortresses in this asbestos enriched soil. They shoveled it, dug it, threw it at each other, made connections containing it, and did all the other things that children normally do. I doubt that any feasible barrier short of 24 hour guard would succeed in keeping children off this dump. And that's what happened. We weren't told. I'm 25 now and I could just picture when I'm 35, having a doctor say, Ms. Carter, you have cancer. I could have that fiber in me and then later I'm going to find out. I have nieces and nephews who are exposed to this and it's sad and we need to do something about it. Thank you. (Stacy Carter, resident of West Ambler, Pennsylvania)

I live in a contaminated community that has two Superfund sites and do you know how hard it is to come here and be away from my community? It's very hard. . . . I'd much rather be with my people of color, indigenous people, urban Indians, Chicanos, and African-American people are all in my community. I live in the oldest community in the South Broadway Corridor [of Albuquerque]. I've been told that I'm very emotional. I feel for everybody out there. And if we can do something to help, we'd like to help. . . . I just wanted to say that this is very difficult to sit here and listen to this because I live it everyday. I'm in the trenches! I'm in the battlefield! (Delores Herrera, NEJAC member from New Mexico)[10]

I wanted to say that I'm in the same shoes with the rest of you all. I'm here trying to make a difference. Where I live I call it a toxic doughnut because I'm surrounded by so many things. But one thing I want to let you know, this is heartbreaking for me also, hearing these complaints. My husband died of lung cancer. I have a son who now might be dying, he has a lung problem, and every time I hear he is asking about insurance payments. He's 40 years old. So I can understand your story. I'm sorry. My son could die any day. Every day, we're smelling all kinds of odors, chemical odors, garbage odors, the sewage treatment plant, everything that you could mention. That's why I'm here today to tell you all, to let you all know that you're not by yourself. I have a big problem. It hurts to hear my son talk about death at such a young age." (Hazel Johnson, NEJAC member and founder of the Chicago-based People for Community Recovery)

The Challenge of Response

These remarks dramatize in a direct and compelling way some of the difficulties facing not only government officials and politicians but also the environmental justice movement itself. What constitutes a reasonable official response to such an array of beliefs and grievances? And is any item on this collective agenda more worthy of prompt and aggressive government action than any other? Such questions are troubling because they are in the end unavoidable, because players in the environmental justice game face continuing incentives to avoid them, and because nothing so constrained as environmental policy can possibly produce the full range of responses and improvements desired.

Quick and effective response to a collective fear is often elusive unless a problem easily meshes with a set of preexisting authorities, resources, and response routines. Ordinary house fires and many natural disasters fit this category, as do outbreaks of many relatively common and well-understood infectious diseases.[11] So do the relatively small, acute hazardous waste threats that qualify for "emergency removal"—widely considered the most successful part of the federal Superfund program.[12]

Added complexity retards effective action. The policy system's default responses in the face of complexity, uncertainty, and limited resources will often be hesitancy, half-measures, and further study, all of which may seem evasive and inadequate to desperate, fearful citizens.[13] And since "the public" and "the experts" tend to perceive very different worlds of risk in the first place, agencies might wind up alienating citizens by throwing expert arguments their way.[14]

It may strike residents, especially in struggling minority or low-income communities, as unresponsive or even callous to point out that factors other than pollution may underlie the health effects they see. For example, it might appear mean-spirited rather than helpful to observe that the death of Hazel Johnson's husband from lung cancer at age forty-one might have had more to do with his cigarette smoking than with ambient industrial pollution. "Although he smoked, I was certain cigarettes didn't kill my husband," she told a reporter not long before her emotional statement at the NEJAC meeting. "He was far too young and much too light of a smoker. There had to be another reason, but at the time I didn't have any idea how to find and prove it." While any causal link between pollution and her husband's premature death must remain speculative, the effect of his death is clear. In 1982, galvanized by a news report suggesting a high cancer rate in her neighborhood, Mrs. Johnson launched a grassroots group, the People for Community Recovery, to press for long overdue repairs at Altgeld Gardens, the public housing development where she lived.[15] Ultimately, the group would tackle the larger "toxic doughnut" of facilities surrounding her neighborhood.[16] The vexing problem facing regulators and politicians is that the perceptions of people like Mrs. Johnson, and their collective intuition about what afflicts their communities, are both genuine and strongly felt. These feelings and perceptions must be taken into account even though they may overstate, sometimes considerably, the local health risks and impacts attributable to pollution.

Information can be both a powerful tool for citizens and a source of controversy. Perhaps the best example in environmental policy is right-to-know legislation, especially the 1986 federal law mandating the Toxics Release Inventory (TRI), which a prominent information resource on local environments describes as "one of the most important advances in information policy since the Freedom of Information Act."[17] Under TRI communities have ample (though by no means complete) firm-specific information regarding transfer and release into the environment of hundreds of chemicals, and thus a potent weapon in the effort to force pollution prevention. Not surprisingly, the community-right-to-know concept has been controversial from the start. Manufacturing interests predictably resisted it on the grounds that providing the information was burdensome, that trade secrets might be endangered, and that citizens would be unable to interpret the information appropriately.[18]

The TRI experience notwithstanding, there are many pitfalls and hurdles attending the effective democratic empowerment of ordinary citizens in regulatory processes.[19] The most fundamental systemic challenge, readily apparent even on theoretical grounds, is the generally superior position (in both participatory resources and incentives) of vested economic interests. Often before proposals are embodied in bills, *Federal Register* notices, or permit applications (and sometimes even before anything exists in written form), business representatives have had informal opportunities to telegraph their views. In many instances, business will have initiated proposals. Considerable information and influence easily flows to such participants. By contrast, channels of focused public involvement tend to be weaker and to be activated later.

The Power of Activism

The experience of the past two decades clearly suggests that communities of all kinds often enjoy ample capacity to block and negotiate changes in projects that stir community objections.[20] Whatever might have been true in prior eras, environmental justice activists cannot claim that communities of color are today unable to effectively challenge projects of which they disapprove. Indeed, the episodes regularly highlighted as examples of injustice often portray projects either blocked outright or substantially transformed to address community concerns. The latter is clearly what happened, for example, in New York City when a group called West Harlem Environmental Action led an effort to challenge the siting of the federally funded North River Water Pollution Control Plant. The plant was built but the community ultimately extracted concessions that included close monitoring, "strict enforcement of certain corrective actions by the State and City," and a $1.1 million North River Fund "to be administered solely by [West Harlem Environmental Action and the Natural Resources Defense Council] and used to address a range of community environmental and public health issues in West Harlem."[21] It is worth recalling that even the landmark 1982 Warren County, North Carolina, battle against a landfill for soil contaminated with polychlorinated biphenyls (PCB) ended with the community securing promises of immunity from further sitings and continued monitoring. It also generated ongoing local activism tied to the PCB issue.[22] Time and again, the environmental justice movement's litany of siting horrors turns out, on closer inspection, to contain many complete and partial successes, including instances where affected individuals are offered substantial compensation and buyouts.

In 1993 the Louisiana Advisory Committee to the U.S. Commission on Civil Rights reviewed seven local environmental justice controversies in the state, involving a total of eight communities (one controversy spanned two communities).[23] In 1986 some residents of Revilletown filed suit, alleging property damage and personal injury from emissions by the Georgia Gulf Corporation, a manufacturer of chemicals and plastics. Residents won relocation and cash settlements. Over a period of years, facing ongoing criticism for offensive odors and claims of adverse health impacts, the Placid Refining Company compensated residents of Sunrise for their property. Dow Chemical did the same for residents of Morrisonville. North of Baton Rouge, in the town of Alsen, residents using a combination of legal action and community organizing received financial concessions and successfully opposed an application by the nation's fourth largest commercial hazardous waste facility to burn PCBs. In 1992 in the town of Wallace the Formosa Chemicals and Fibre Corporation was blocked in its attempt to build a rayon and wood pulp processing plant. With considerable outside help, citizens of Willow Springs effectively mobilized to challenge

Browning-Ferris Industries Chemical Services over its management of a hazardous waste site. And a proposed uranium enrichment plant in Claiborne parish, to be operated by Louisiana Energy Services (LES), was successfully challenged by local activists and the Sierra Club Legal Defense Fund.[24]

While all took place within a single state's boundaries, these Louisiana cases vary, with each unfolding as a complicated story often spanning many years. The controversies often left a residue of bitterness among some residents who resented that their communities had faced unpleasant choices and sometimes complete uprooting with its attendant disruption. Emotions sometimes ran high as company promises of much-needed jobs, and the lure of settlement offers, drove a wedge among residents. But at the very least these cases clearly portray communities far removed from the helpless victims of movement lore. Effective use of such tools as community organizing, lawsuits, press coverage, and alliances with sophisticated and sympathetic outsiders—belie the image of helplessness. In no case did overwhelmed residents wind up with little or nothing to show for their interaction with the firms in question. While the outcomes may not have been everyone's idea of "environmental justice," they do not add up to the advisory committee's idea of "environmental racism" either.[25]

A good example of activism's power is the town of Chester, Pennsylvania, on behalf of which Zulene Mayfield had tearfully testified during the January 1995 NEJAC meeting. By the time of her December 1996 NEJAC appearance, Mayfield was visibly more upbeat, and with good reason. Chester Residents Concerned for Quality Living had succeeded in bringing a lawsuit against the Commonwealth of Pennsylvania and in attracting substantial state and national media attention to its cause.[26] EPA regional administrator Peter Kostmayer, a former Democratic member of Congress, had taken an interest in Chester, as had activists from several colleges and universities who comprised the Campus Coalition Concerning Contamination, which was targeting its energies on the town. Key polluters had taken notice and one had shut down. Mayfield had brought with her to the NEJAC meeting a documentary videotape depicting the struggle of residents to rid themselves of the many environmental assaults they faced. As she spoke, NEJAC activists were visibly pleased, even proud. Zulene Mayfield was a vivid example of what determined citizens could achieve.

Barnstorming and Brainstorming: EPA and Community Involvement

Efforts to stimulate ongoing and meaningful public involvement in regulatory policy processes clearly face significant problems, especially when fear and outrage are muted. Sheer nonparticipation, resulting in nonrepresentativeness, is exceedingly difficult to address. "No matter what the circumstances, many who are eligible to participate do not," observes John Clayton Thomas in a recent prescriptive overview of public involvement, "and those who do participate are seldom a cross section of all who are eligible."[27] This is especially true where persons of low income and education are concerned; in particular, the correlation between propensity to participate in politics and level of education is well established.[28]

The EPA has provided considerable advisory access for committed activists but struggles when trying to cast a wider net effectively. Such efforts can often yield indifference, alienation, or torrents of ill-informed and unfocused anger. As President Clinton was about to sign executive order 12898 in February 1994, seven agencies, including the EPA and the National Institute of Environmental Health Sciences, sponsored a Symposium on Health Research and Needs to Ensure Environmental Justice at an Arlington, Virginia, hotel.[29] According to an EPA official who helped arrange it, one intention of organizers was to reach beyond the regular coterie of "activists who come to everything," bringing in "ordinary folks" from communities around the country. A $300,000 government subsidy helped generate some 1,300 attendees, nearly twice as many as had been expected.[30] But the event is still grimly recalled less for any initiatives it generated than for the harsh questioning and verbal attacks that reduced EPA administrator Browner to tears when she departed from her prepared remarks and conversed with the assembly in a prolonged and unscripted series of exchanges.

More generally, large participatory meetings are often unwieldy and prone to theatrics. Evidence suggests that any effect of even orderly public hearings on established federal programs may be small and temporary, if there is any effect at all.[31] Focus is bound to be particularly elusive when representatives of multiple communities attend or set the agenda. In the environmental justice context, such meetings emanate from, and sustain, the belief that all concerns deserve redress—an inclusiveness that appeals both ideologically, because it allows advocates to escape the role of "victimizer," and politically, because it avoids potentially divisive battles over the movement's agenda.

As noted earlier, local agendas tend to animate local groups, and it is inherently difficult to build a coalition among such groups except by embracing everyone's parochial concerns. Such groups are often institutionally fragile; they have few resources and notoriously rely on a small core of reliable activists.[32] Once the immediate threat that mobilized the group has passed, persons who have contributed vital organizational resources may drift away. Many organizations may sustain themselves over the long run largely through external (for example, foundation) support and by eschewing political advocacy altogether in favor of a service focus.[33]

Despite such hurdles, generating effective citizen involvement remains at the heart of the Clinton administration's environmental justice commitment. The administration is pursuing what might be called "insider" and "outsider" approaches to increasing sensitivity for the concerns of underrepresented groups (meaning, for the most part, racial minorities) in environmental decisionmaking. Faced with demands for response, officials have found a relatively safe haven in varieties of consultative—but, again, not authoritative—citizen participation: advisory boards, public forums, community outreach efforts, and access to information (with due regard for readers and speakers of Spanish). By stressing nonbinding mechanisms of inclusion and the vague prospect for empowerment through the dissemination and use of technical knowledge, officials pay homage to democratic values, signal benign intent, and hope to deflect criticism. Citizen advisory bodies and community outreach efforts try to bring aboard government "outsiders." On the other hand, the government's effort to provide greater opportunity for administrative review of local complaints, designation of an internal EPA Office of Environmental Justice (OEJ) and environmental justice coordinators in EPA regional offices, and long-range pursuit of workforce diversity are all intended to create presumably sympathetic "insiders." Taken together these mechanisms do not spring from any clear theory of what environmental justice requires but instead from advocacy, administrative soul-searching, and incremental groping on multiple fronts, since public involvement is very much a "work in progress." Because it is widely assumed that the pursuit of environmental justice must be multifaceted, and because each of these approaches is plausible, defensible, and mostly noncontroversial, it is not surprising that they have all been pursued.

The OEJ and NEJAC are the primary institutional initiatives the EPA has offered to address exclusion and the unfairness presumed to stem from it. The OEJ serves as "the point of contact for environmental justice outreach and educational activities, provides technical and financial assistance, and disseminates environmental justice information."[34] The OEJ and NEJAC function in tandem; the OEJ provides administrative support to the council, while the director of the OEJ serves on NEJAC as the "designated federal official" required under the NEJAC charter.[35] Taken together these bodies serve not only the professed goal of inclusion but also as an institutional defense apparatus for the EPA—a combination of political armor (to ward off attacks) and steam valve (to channel pressure safely). Activists are probably aware, if only intuitively, of such aspects in the institutional milieu. Yet they have little practical choice but to play the game, trying all the while to nudge it as far as possible in a preferred direction.

NEJAC began its work in a controversy that, although resolved by the second council meeting, reflects tensions underlying its relationship with the EPA and the inclination of activists to view government bureaucracies with suspicion. Even before the first council meeting in May 1994, activists on NEJAC were pressing for greater autonomy and assurances of institutional integrity. EPA administrator Carol Browner had created NEJAC as a body of up to twenty-five members, designated four subcommittees, and appointed John Hall, chairman of the Texas Natural Resources Conservation Commission, as NEJAC chair.

Activists on the council—as distinct from business community members—immediately wanted changes. In a letter dated nine days before the first meeting, a dozen members complained that only twenty-three council positions had been filled, despite the absence of representation by important groups and constituencies. Moreover the activists wanted the council to create its own subcommittees and to get rid of Hall as chair. "We also understand," wrote the activists, "that there are several environmental discrimination lawsuits pending against Mr. Hall and the Commission he chairs. We feel that it would be inappropriate and a possible conflict of interest for any sitting . . . member . . . to chair the body who has a pending environmental discrimination lawsuit."[36] The issue continued through the next council meeting in August 1994, where Hall, facing an adverse vote of the council membership, agreed to step aside. As his replacement the activists united behind one of their own, Richard Moore of the Southwest Network for Environmental and Economic Justice. Jovial, down-to-earth, and clearly committed to an activist perspective, Moore proved a popular chairman until the end of his tenure in 1997, when he departed the council. He was succeeded by Haywood Turrentine, an Alabama-based labor activist.

Activist members also made sure that they could outmaneuver business representatives on the council if need be. Decisions would be made by majority vote rather than by consensus, as some industry representatives urged.[37]

With its largely activist membership, its six subcommittees (including about sixty-five members, most of whom are not full NEJAC members), and ample time set aside for public comment, NEJAC regularly offers a platform for voices, like those of Zulene Mayfield and Hazel Johnson, that might otherwise be absent, or less resonant, in EPA proceedings. In reality, all six subcommittees share de facto responsibility for "public participation and accountability" even though only one bears the formal title. By 1997 one of the council's most significant products was its *Model Plan for Public Participation* pamphlet, published in November 1996, a document announced as intended to be "reviewed annually and revised as necessary."[38]

Its relatively congenial and accessible structure belies two basic limitations. One is that, like the environmental justice movement that inspired it, NEJAC is unable to define or focus on a set of policy priorities smaller than the full universe of federal, state, and local environmental justice issues. Painstakingly participatory in orientation, hopping among issues as they arise and ideas as they are generated, the council is a mechanism appropriate to conveying, and perhaps amplifying, demands, but not for deciding which ones deserve priority or how they should be compromised on behalf of other goals. Like the October 1991 First National People of Color Environmental Leadership Summit, which yielded its seventeen principles of environmental justice through political and highly ideological accumulation rather than discriminating analysis, NEJAC is not the place to look for hard thinking about the boundaries of, or potential tradeoffs embedded in, environmental justice. The prevailing council view appears to be that all communities and all voices within them are more or less equally legitimate and deserving. Accordingly, their main concern is to enhance the overall "community presence" whenever and wherever possible. That, for example, is why the council successfully prodded the EPA to allow the creation of an indigenous peoples subcommittee in 1995; several NEJAC members had long been concerned that "issues important to indigenous peoples had not been addressed adequately by the existing committee structure of NEJAC."[39] The council listens sympathetically to public comments and encourages the EPA or other agencies to take action. Its focus, especially within its subcommittees, is less on health or risk than on ferreting out and elevating community perspectives. But NEJAC eschews anything like a formal comparative assessment among the claims brought before it and there is no pressure from the EPA, or from anywhere else for that matter, for it to behave otherwise.

Not surprisingly, NEJAC's determination to achieve maximum inclusiveness can be procedurally debilitating at times. For example, in December 1996, at NEJAC's eighth meeting in Baltimore, the public comment calendar was overcrowded, as is often the case; more than thirty individuals were signed up to speak. Chairman Moore, as usual, gently and repeatedly reminded both council members and the public of the "need to move along" to get through the list. But then a pair of Native American activists offered a rambling joint presentation that ended by calling for NEJAC to help free imprisoned activist Leonard Peltier, whom many observers have long believed to have been unjustly convicted for the murder of two FBI agents. The flow of public comment immediately halted as various council members (including chairman Moore) offered damning opinions regarding Peltier's incarceration. As the council began discussing what action it might appropriately take, no one dared venture what might appear obvious: that whatever the merits of Peltier's case, an EPA advisory council was simply an inappropriate forum in which to address that issue.

The council's other fundamental limitation lies in its absence of authority and highly restricted institutional capacity. Though some members have been quite knowledgeable about aspects of environmental policy (especially environmental law), NEJAC is not an expert review committee in the mold of those on which the National Institutes of Health and the Food and Drug Administration, respectively, rely to allocate research funds and evaluate new products.[40] NEJAC relies on technical expertise available from the EPA and other agencies, assistance offered regularly at full council and subcommittee meetings. But NEJAC cannot evaluate the reliability of presentations made to it by experts or citizens. (As one member put it: "We aren't fact-finders.") Nor can it intervene decisively in issues brought before it. Instead, the council's twice-yearly meetings, supplemented by considerable interim communication, offer opportunities for interested laypersons to elevate and ventilate information and issues brought before them (including, on occasion, issues over which the EPA may have little influence). Lacking any "line" role, NEJAC can shape EPA policies only indirectly, by commenting on drafts of documents, such as the various agency environmental justice strategies mandated by the executive order or proposed revisions of administrative guidance on enforcement of the National Environmental Policy Act.[41] It can encourage the EPA to "look into" something and monitor further developments at future meetings but little more.

Activists were aware at the outset of severe constraints on NEJAC's usefulness. Indeed, some were unhappy to see it created at all, preferring something closer to the informal access they believed they had achieved under Browner's predecessor. "When we proposed [an advisory committee] we didn't propose it as a solution but as a tactic to keep some 'juice' in the system," recalled one prominent activist who later served on the council. "I thought that each of these subcommittees would come up with recommendations that the agency would massage into their own initiatives."[42] Some activists were also dubious about creating the OEJ, fearing that its existence would institutionally marginalize environmental justice within the EPA. It is, to be sure, awkwardly situated. Created in 1992 as the Office of Environmental Equity near the end of the Bush administration, the office lay outside both the EPA's main environmental media (air, water, hazardous waste) and enforcement units.

During 1995 the OEJ became part of the Office of Enforcement and Compliance Assurance (OECA), headed by EPA assistant administrator Steve Herman. Sympathetic to the desire of minority communities and environmental justice advocates to gain a secure foothold in the administrative process, and well aware of the enormous access advantage enjoyed by business interests, Herman wanted to ensure OEJ of a safe haven in the EPA bureaucracy. As he later told Congress, he also believed that housing the OEJ inside OECA would facilitate addressing environmental justice efforts on an integrated, multimedia basis.[43] Herman attended NEJAC meetings, and even its subcommittee sessions, where he held reassuring and informative dialogues with members. In line with the position taken by EPA administrator Browner, Herman pledged that his

office would make environmental justice an ongoing concern, routinely integrated into OECA's activities, both at headquarters and in
the field. For example, after EPA's Region 6 office sponsored an
October 1996 enforcement roundtable in San Antonio, Texas, for discussion among activists, industry representatives, and government
officials, Herman decided that each EPA region should sponsor such
an event.[44] However, achieving sustained integration of environmental justice into EPA enforcement will require far more than good
intentions at the top. A multitude of political and bargaining considerations, policy tradeoffs, and case-specific variations apply in
enforcement. It is also a realm where substantial operational-level
discretion challenges even determined management efforts.[45]
Clearly, Herman had his work cut out for him.

Facilitating outreach and informed participation is also a core
task for the regional environmental justice coordinators. This was
evident at the July 1995 NEJAC meeting, as nine of these coordinators briefed the council on their activities. James Younger of
Region 1 (New England) "urged EPA to recognize the community's ability to make decisions and let communities define the
kind of ecosystems protection they want. EPA then should team
with communities to address the protection of urban ecosystems."[46] The coordinator from Region 4 (the Deep South) noted
that the regional administrator and managers below him had been
devoting a significant amount of time to meeting with community
groups.[47] Region 7 (Iowa, Kansas, Missouri, and Nebraska) was
about to stage its first environmental justice summit.[48]

The EPA tries to put at least small amounts of money where its
mouth is. The OEJ oversees and promotes two grant programs
intended to upgrade the information base enjoyed by local community groups, along with their ability to address local issues effectively. To encourage partnerships between institutions of higher
learning and local residents, the EPA has operated a community-
university partnership grant program offering up to $250,000 for up
to three years for six partnerships.[49] (At the December 1997 NEJAC
meeting the EPA announced that funding for the program would be
suspended in 1998).[50] And in June 1993, OEJ began running a small

grants program that, in fiscal year 1996, awarded $3,000,000 to 150 organizations.[51] Facilitating community involvement, information gathering, and coordination are the goals of the program. Regional offices reported that they have been using small grants to community organizations to stimulate public participation. In Region 8 (Colorado, Montana, North and South Dakota, Utah, and Wyoming) more than half the grants had been awarded to Native American organizations, and Region 9 (which includes California) had allocated $50,000 in the vicinity of a Superfund site.[52]

All this amounts to a process that might roughly be summarized as "barnstorming and brainstorming." That is, the OEJ along with NEJAC, its subcommittees, and EPA's ten regional offices are collectively casting about for involvement by, feedback from, and sometimes even "partnership" with a variety of groups and communities, seeking to promote their continued engagement and to generate ideas about how their many concerns might be addressed. The EPA and NEJAC barnstorm the country through announcements, meetings, and other kinds of community contact, and through promises of assistance in procuring useful information.

The real work of most meetings, aside from airing community grievances, consists largely of brainstorming for ways both to prod the government toward a stronger environmental justice position and to put existing policy tools more generally at the service of communities of color. At its December 1996 meeting in Baltimore, for example, NEJAC's enforcement subcommittee mulled over such matters as how the EPA might use (and be prompted to use) Title VI of the Civil Rights Act (see below); its potential influence over local permitting; and its power to negotiate Supplemental Environmental Projects (SEPs)—all in the service of environmental justice.[53]

The EPA's Office of Solid Waste and Emergency Response (OSWER) has similarly emphasized public involvement in building support for its emerging brownfields redevelopment initiative. When OSWER deputy assistant administrator Tim Fields broached the brownfields concept at an Atlanta NEJAC meeting in January 1995, activists were skeptical. The agency, explained Fields, essentially wanted to use its administrative discretion to reduce barriers

to development inadvertently created by the liability fears surrounding Superfund (see chapter 5). Throughout the 1980s and
1990s Superfund was proving a local economic albatross; developers, insurers, and lending institutions shunned involvement in these
"brownfields"—properties and projects having potential cleanup
liability entanglements. Activists present at Fields's presentation,
such as Charles Lee of the United Church of Christ, Commission for
Racial Justice, were initially concerned about where the balance of
power might lie in brownfields implementation. Would communities be adequately consulted? Would some locales have to settle for
riskier land uses than might otherwise be available?[54] Another
NEJAC member interviewed later chided brownfields as a "very
top-down" approach and thus inherently suspect.

The EPA attempted to address such concerns largely through a
demonstrated commitment to vigorous "dialogue" and community
participation in the brownfields program. In the spring of 1995, aware
of the cool reception the brownfields concept had received at the
Atlanta NEJAC meeting, OSWER began planning a series of "loop
trips" to Detroit, Philadelphia, and other cities to address suspicions
among community activists that the EPA was only interested in feedback from the business community. The EPA's efforts, and assiduous
cultivation of activists like Lee, paid off. By the time the EPA and
HUD sponsored a major brownfields conference in Pittsburgh in
September 1996, many activists were largely supportive.[55]

In embracing public participation for the brownfields initiative,
OSWER was following a course charted earlier for Superfund more
generally. As the Northeast-Midwest Institute observed recently:

> Public involvement is given brief mention in CERCLA Section 117, in
> which EPA is directed to offer communities affected by NPL
> [National Priorities List] sites the opportunity to comment after
> cleanup remedies are proposed, after the original remedy chosen is
> altered for some reason, and when a Consent Decree is available for
> public review. Numerous complaints by local residents affected by
> Superfund site cleanups have helped EPA understand the need for
> early, thorough, and ongoing community involvement in virtually all

decisions regarding site cleanups and reuse. As a matter of principle, the agency has sought over the past several years to expand opportunities for public hearings, disseminate site information to broader cross-sections of the communities, and present understandable information on risks associated with alternative remedy selections.[56]

Public Involvement Outside the EPA

The EPA is only one part of the federal government where a focus on inclusion took hold pursuant to executive order 12898. The formal environmental justice strategies produced by other agencies and departments demonstrate this. The Nuclear Regulatory Commission and the Departments of Agriculture, Defense, and Interior all highlighted "public participation and outreach" in their strategies. Interior's document particularly indicates how central the inclusion focus is to environmental justice. The department identified four environmental justice goals and placed participation at the top of the list: "the Department will involve minority and low income communities as we make environmental decisions and assure public access to our environmental information."[57] Goal number two would be to "provide its employees environmental justice guidance and *with the help of minority and low-income communities* develop training which will reduce their exposure to environmental health and safety hazards"; goal number four promised *"public partnership opportunities"* with various stakeholders in the service of environmental justice.[58] Thus, in a document ostensibly articulating four separate goals, the pledge of community involvement overwhelms or underlies three—all but the goal of enhanced research and data collection.

Other agencies promised, as had the EPA, to make use of existing advisory council mechanisms. At Interior, for example, the Fish and Wildlife Service required that minority and disadvantaged individuals be included on councils advising recipients of agency funds, while the Office of Surface Mining (OSM) established an advisory board to "consist of representatives from OSM's constituent groups . . . [with] Native Americans and citizens in the coal fields . . . [having] a direct link with the Director of OSM in airing and resolving concerns."[59]

In a similar vein, the Defense Department promised that a primary vehicle for inclusion would be local Restoration Advisory Boards (RABs). The Defense Department's environmental justice strategy describes RABs as "the cornerstone of [department] efforts to expand community involvement in decisions about cleanup at military bases. By bringing together people who reflect the many diverse interests within the community, a RAB can help identify issues of concern and reduce potential communication problems that could result in needless delays."[60] The department also issued an August 1994 guidance document requiring that "each RAB reflect the diversity of the communities in which RABs operate."[61] At Defense, as at the EPA and elsewhere, participation was to be essentially consultative rather than authoritative and presumably subject to the various pitfalls and limitations affecting citizen participation generally. Moreover, a truly representative RAB emerging out of any community with significant ethnic and class diversity might not have sufficient ethnic minority presence to count for much in the end.

For most agencies, environmental justice may largely mean performing activities that would have seemed necessary to some extent even without an executive order. Clearly some environmental officials in progressive states like California believe that they have, as one put it, "already been doing environmental justice" (through more general efforts at citizen outreach) but without using the trendy new label. The Clinton initiative may have the effect of leading agencies toward a somewhat heightened procedural sensitivity, and more aggressive public relations, than would otherwise have been apparent. Listening to and responding to specific constituencies is, after all, at the heart of a number of departmental and agency missions. Interior and Agriculture must deal with Native American tribes anyway, and such departments can readily adopt working definitions of environmental justice that are quite compatible with their more general mandates and histories.

At an agency without such a clientele focus, like the National Aeronautics and Space Administration (NASA), environmental justice can easily be interpreted to mean something like "being as sensitive as possible to the concerns and social textures of the communities adjacent to our operations." For example, Ames Research Center, a NASA wind-test facility in San Jose, California, is near a low-income mobile home park, where noise has been a concern. Through a proactive mail campaign and extensive community contact, NASA was able to smooth its relations with residents.[62] The National Regulatory Commission [NRC] held its first post-executive order outreach effort at a "pre-scoping" meeting in Sequoia Fields, Oklahoma, site of a proposed facility closing. Under the National Environmental Policy Act the NRC was already required to hold a "scoping" meeting early in its environmental assessment process.[63] But with environmental justice in mind, the NRC went beyond the NEPA regulations to hold a "pre-scoping" meeting explicitly to solicit involvement from low-income and minority persons in particular.[64]

Legal Tools: Title VI and NEPA

No single mechanism for giving communities greater leverage in the name of environmental justice has attracted more attention or stimulated more discussion than Title VI of the Civil Rights Act of 1964.[65] This provision of federal law states: "No person in the United States shall, on the ground of race, color, or national origin, be excluded from participation in, be denied the benefits of, or be subjected to discrimination under any program or activity receiving Federal financial assistance." The presidential memorandum accompanying the executive order includes a paragraph that identifies and paraphrases Title VI specifically, virtually inviting agencies and activists to pursue it as an avenue of redress.[66] The EPA is currently wrestling internally with the question of how Title VI might be made to serve environmental justice purposes.

Title VI originally emerged as a focus of debate and advocacy largely because of the widespread failure of environmental justice litigation grounded in the equal protection clause of the Constitution.[67] A key obstacle has been that Supreme Court equal protection doctrine developed in the 1970s such that plaintiffs must go beyond a showing of racially discriminatory impact, proving discriminatory intent on the part of the defendant.[68] This is a very high standard to meet, as James H. Colopy observes: "To prove discriminatory intent, however, a plaintiff must show that the defendant acted with a racially discriminatory purpose in mind. . . . [This is] a difficult burden that few have been able to meet."[69]

But as a former NEJAC member, law professor Richard Lazarus points out, Title VI is not shackled by similar judicial interpretation. "The principal advantage of Title VI over equal protection," writes Lazarus, "is that courts have not required a showing of discriminatory intent in the Title VI context: disparate impact has been enough."[70] Lazarus goes on to suggest that "EPA has not exploited its Title VI responsibilities as it could to redress distributional inequities."[71] The agency could, suggests Lazarus, require that recipients of federal funds formally show that the money is being distributed in a racially neutral manner, or perhaps even that racial minorities be "proportionately represented among the ultimate beneficiaries of the federal funds."[72] One obvious problem with this latter suggestion would be its tendency to hamper the EPA's ability to direct funds where they are most needed in light of other, arguably more compelling, policy criteria, such as public health impact.

That concern aside, however, Title VI has some clear practical limits. First, it is useful only if the target entity is a recipient of federal funds.[73] Its effective use also depends on complaints being both timely and carefully crafted; they must contain appropriate allegations and sufficient factual support. These are requirements that many potential grassroots complainants—strapped for resources and unaccustomed to the rigors of formal legal process—will be unable to meet. At a May 1996 NEJAC meeting in Detroit, staff of the EPA Office of Civil Rights (OCR) reported that of thirty complaints that had been filed, twelve had been rejected and one withdrawn for one or more of the weaknesses cited above.[74] Another problem has been limited agency resources. As of mid-1996 OCR's external compliance program had only four full-time equivalent employees (FTEs) available to investigate Title VI complaints.

By 1998 no one had yet succeeded in bringing, and winning, a substantive Title VI environmental justice case in court, although the residents of Chester, Pennsylvania, did prevail in a 1997 federal circuit court on the question of their right to sue under Title VI.[75] As of 1994 California advocacy lawyer Luke W. Cole (who would join NEJAC in 1996) had personal knowledge of only one case, involving the siting of a freeway in Durham, North Carolina, as a local Title VI legal victory. In a 1986 negotiated settlement the state agreed to reroute a freeway and modify an interchange to preserve a church and park.[76] Indeed, the Center on Race, Poverty and the Environment, where Cole serves as general counsel, generally advises against lawsuits in environmental justice siting disputes, because they are both hard to win (especially with traditional civil rights legal tools) and a potential distraction from the underlying political and economic struggles that communities need to wage.[77] Cole is quite explicit that even *losing* cases may be useful in helping communities mobilize, generate media attention, and pressure key elites:

> Bringing a civil rights suit against local government officials can be very satisfying for the community group involved, because it calls the problem what it is: a violation of civil rights. It is one high-profile way of saying that the official being sued is engaging in racist practices. This act alone makes such suits worthwhile to some groups with long-term experiences with racist decision-makers—filing a suit allows a community to say "officially" what has existed for a long time, and builds morale within the group.[78]

Cole makes transparent that, for many activists, environmental justice is mostly about accountability and political power rather than the more technical issue of environmental risks facing communities. A major reason why one simply cannot accept advocacy claims of risk at face value is that they are often anchored, ultimately, not in the dangers posed by a site or substance ostensibly at issue, but rather in a desire for transformed power relationships to be achieved on behalf of politically energized and engaged communities. When activists seek reduced barriers for local Title VI claims, they are essentially engaged in the same game that Benjamin Chavis and the Commission for Racial Justice were playing with *Toxic Wastes and Race in the United States*.[79]

Debate over Title VI as an environmental justice tool greatly intensified in 1998. Throughout the spring, many state environmental authorities and business groups reacted harshly to proposed EPA guidance for investigating Title VI administrative complaints. Critics assailed the guidance as overly vague, an unnecessary threat to the integrity of state environmental permit programs, and inconsistent with economic development.[80] And then, in June, the United States Supreme Court agreed to decide whether the Chester Residents Concerned for Quality Living could sue the Pennsylvania Department of Environmental Protection for discriminatory impact under the EPA's Title VI regulations.[81] A victory for the Chester residents would be a major movement triumph, setting the stage for much greater reliance on Title VI by community groups.

Another federal statute that both the EPA and activists hope to put more fully to environmental justice uses is the National Environmental Policy Act. Since its passage in 1969 this landmark law has made a key "action-forcing" mechanism—the environmental impact statement (EIS)—one of the central elements in environmental policy implementation throughout the country.[82] Cole and other observers place "traditional" environmental laws like NEPA, and the potential procedural leverage they offer community advocates, at the top of their hierarchy of litigation strategies, especially for blocking unwanted sitings.[83] Like Title VI, NEPA was specifically noted by President Clinton when the executive order was promulgated.[84] Given this, and NEPA's history as a primary tool for both environmentalists and middle-class opponents of local development projects, it is not surprising that NEPA would have attracted attention and serious rumination from the outset of the Clinton administration.

But the administration moved cautiously on NEPA. In lieu of statutory revision there would be a guidance document from the White House Council on Environmental Quality (CEQ), which had oversight responsibility for compliance with both NEPA and the executive order. But CEQ did not release a draft version of its proposed NEPA guidance until May 1996, nearly two and a half years after the issuance of the executive order; the delay was frustrating both to NEJAC and to EPA.[85] The lag stemmed, in the words of the CEQ associate director for toxics and environmental protection, from "the importance of this issue to the Administration as a whole and to the particular programs of a wide range of individual agencies."[86]

The proposed guidance that emerged would be a brief (fourteen pages, plus appendix) and rather general document, as was perhaps inevitable given both the character of NEPA itself and the range of participants doubtless weighing in with specific institutional stakes in mind. The guidance viewed environmental justice very broadly, noting that "environmental justice issues may arise at any step of the NEPA process" and "encompass a broad range of impacts covered by NEPA, including impacts on the natural or physical environment and interrelated social and economic effects." Observing that there was "not a rote formula for how environmental justice issues should be identified or addressed,"[87] the guidance, in line with NEPA itself, invited agencies to be creative about public participation and communication and diligent about impact assessment.

On the other hand, the guidance cautioned, low-income and minority populations could not expect anything like a NEPA equivalent of "hard" affirmative action. "Environmental impact that is not 'significant' within the meaning of NEPA would not be rendered significant simply because an insignificant impact has a disproportionate and adverse effect" on such a population.[88] Moreover, such effects would "not preclude a proposed agency action from going forward, nor necessarily compel a conclusion that a proposed action is environmentally unsatisfactory."[89] Derived from a quintessentially procedural statute, CEQ's NEPA guidance (and a far more detailed document proposed by the EPA in July 1996 for its own NEPA compliance analyses)[90] attempted to encourage agency procedures toward greater sensitivity and accessibility without crossing the line into commitments that specified outcomes would be forthcoming. The extent to which such prodding will work, and the difference it would make, must remain speculative for the present. But effective linkages among social aspirations, procedures embraced to pursue them, and desired social outcomes are often undermined in policymaking. In this instance those linkages are obviously vulnerable to the facts of concrete local circumstances, to limitations inherent in procedural tools, to more specific substantive mandates embedded in environmental legislation, and to larger regime characteristics (especially markets and enduring macro- and micro-level political understandings).

Environmental Justice and the Politics of Inclusion

In American politics few will fault "fairness" or "community involvement" as values, but designing specific institutional vehicles to pursue them is a politically tender enterprise. Environmental justice as a cause arose in the 1980s and emerged on the federal policy agenda in the 1990s, timing that tended to constrain the substantive response that might be forthcoming. Environmental policy was already well developed, and the larger regime was in no mood for legislative tinkering on behalf of this new concern. Most siting lay in the hands of state and local authorities in any case, and it was not clear what incentives and penalties could or would be deployed by the federal government at those levels of government in the service of environmental justice. Although many observers deeply sensed that disproportionate burdens existed, there was no consensus on what those burdens entailed, on the nature of their consequences, or on how to provide relief.

Everyone could agree that there existed considerable grassroots anger, that there were places (epitomized by Chester, Pennsylvania) where environmental "disamenities" visibly challenged the local quality of life, and that many communities were nothing like full partners in determining the use of their public spaces. Furthermore, the racial minorities that constituted most of the environmental justice movement—African Americans, non-Cuban Latinos, and Native Americans—were crucial elements in the Democratic Party's (and President Clinton's) electoral coalition. Environmental justice would at the very least be good symbolic politics that would not further strain an already tight fiscal situation.

Given this combination of considerations, the creative use of administrative discretion to propel community involvement in policymaking proved a politically feasible path. It is telling that the proposed Environmental Justice Act offered by then-senator Al Gore in 1992—a bill that could have led to the tough step of banning new pollution sources in particularly burdened areas—was nowhere to be found as Vice President Gore became the Clinton administration's chief environmental policy guru the following year.

In light of all this, reliance on the executive order mechanism was an obvious option for the Clinton administration. Presidents rely on executive orders as a relatively uncontested way to instruct the bureaucracy, and sometimes to make largely symbolic appeals, without expending the time or political capital necessary to undertake legislative battles that may be unwinnable. (Prolonged contests may arise subsequently, as the legendary Truman order to desegregate the military and the Reagan orders on regulatory relief attest.)[91]

Executive order 12160, promulgated by President Jimmy Carter in September 1979 to facilitate consumer involvement in policymaking, is perhaps worth recalling.[92] The Carter order directed that "agencies shall establish procedures for the early and meaningful participation by consumers in the development and review of all agency rules, policies, and programs."[93] The Carter order also established a Consumer Affairs Council, an interdepartmental oversight body very similar to the Interagency Working Group created by the Clinton order. The Carter White House had been searching for a way to champion consumerism after seeing its proposed Consumer Protection Agency, intended to institutionalize such advocacy as a formal part of the federal government, defeated in Congress in the spring of 1978.[94] The executive order proved a politically viable if substantively rather inert mechanism (and one quickly overtaken by Carter's defeat for reelection). It is doubtful that the structure created could have yielded much even in a second Carter term.

The prospects for the executive order on environmental justice are somewhat brighter, and not just because Clinton won the second term that eluded Carter. EPA's leadership is regularly vocal on the subject. The grassroots fear and anger that propelled the issue onto the federal agenda remains. The movement's allies among churches and universities rally in opposition to environmental racism, although it is unclear what significant burdens many are willing or able to bear for the cause.[95] After all, a declaration of fealty to environmental justice, by itself, imposes no real cost on the institution (public or private) offering it. For some, embrace of the label may have more to do with institutional self-image and public relations than with a decision to make environmental justice an active ongoing priority for which precious resources are to be expended. As for the Clinton administration, it remains unclear precisely what the White House and the many federal agencies affected by the executive order are committed to in the long run, beyond a general yearning to listen hard and do good.

4

HEALTH

Rᴇᴅᴜᴄɪɴɢ ᴀɴᴅ ᴀᴠᴏɪᴅɪɴɢ threats to health is a major, but often unproductive, theme of environmental justice advocacy. When activists call attention to alleged unfair environmental burdens, surreptitious mass poisoning is a primary (if sometimes implicit) fear.[1] After all, why care about an inequity unless it makes a difference? And isn't the difference between life and death the biggest difference of all? Given the vehemently articulated community health anxieties evident in countless public forums, including the National Environmental Justice Advisory Council (NEJAC), one might mistakenly conclude that health is the main, or even sole, focus of environmental justice activism.

As is explained in the previous chapter, policymakers and activists alike have tended to concentrate on questions and mechanisms of community involvement, not community health. This is not surprising. One reason for this focus is that activists and policymakers alike possess a far better understanding of procedural inclusion, and of the tools that seem useful for producing it, than they do of ways to reduce risk and enhance health. Moreover, for both activists and policymakers, community involvement speaks in an immediate and direct way

to the political challenge at hand. For activists, involvement offers out-
lets for advocacy, opportunities for dialogue and the casting of blame,
and the promise of institutional accountability. Resourceful and well-
timed advocacy may even lead to significant material benefits for a
community. On the other hand, involvement mechanisms allow
policymakers to exhibit responsiveness and deflect criticism. By comparison, channeling health anxieties effectively toward risk reductions
and improved health prospects among low income and minority persons is far more difficult.

It is not hard to understand why activists are inclined to think
that what they do generally promotes healthy communities. An ability to exercise power, as when a neighborhood effectively mobilizes
to block visible sources of perceived additional risk, strongly implies
a protective capacity. People commonly attribute harm to things
they intensely dislike or fear, such as dumps and pollution. While
both can certainly cause harm, so can many other things not nearly
so fearsome. Moreover, fighting polluters clearly requires collective
action or governmental intervention; rugged individualism cannot
suffice. Only a short and intuitive step separates this basic insight
from the impression that collective triumph over a "polluter" has
salutary effects. Finally, health, wealth, and political efficacy are
clearly correlated; no one would deny that wealthy persons extract
better health care, healthier surroundings, and greater overall solic-
itude from politicians than poor persons.

For these reasons it may appear obvious that successfully exercis-
ing power over environmental questions where health concerns have
been raised is in fact to protect health. When mobilized residents shut
down a facility, prevent its construction, or otherwise force greater
distance between themselves and unwanted sites (by winning relocation of residents or facilities), it is usually seen as a blow struck for
health. But the victory may actually be hollow or insignificant, for the
connection between successful activism and the advancement of public health is much less straightforward than it might appear. In fact
environmental justice advocacy and policymaking might subtly
impede efforts to improve and protect health among precisely those
persons advocates and policymakers desire to help. This can occur if

mechanisms of mobilization and involvement draw citizen concern and protective effort away from important sources of risk (to less important sources) and away from preventable adverse effects (to unpreventable or unsubstantiated ones). Citizen energies thus displaced may complicate the task policymakers must face in allocating scarce resources to their most productive use.

Three principal problems are elaborated in this chapter. First, environmental justice often highlights aspects of the human environment where evidence of serious and continuing harm to human health (and of disproportionate harm to environmental justice constituencies) is weak or ambiguous. The movement's obsession with disproportionate adverse impacts may obscure more important questions relating to the absolute size, scope, and source of such impacts. Second, environmental justice proponents generally eschew personal behavior (and necessary changes in it) as a primary variable in the health of low-income and minority communities. Third, from among the vast array of issues raised to date under the environmental justice rubric, adherents have been incapable of fashioning a coherent agenda of substantive public health priorities. Instead the movement is drawn to an overall procedural priority of citizen involvement, an orientation that unrealistically envisions every issue as a substantive priority.

These limitations exist largely because environmental justice is not mainly a public health movement. It is instead a loose coalition of citizens and groups advocating greater grassroots democracy, usually with an eye fixed on broader social justice goals. Because its primary political aims are to bind residents together, to raise their collective profile in policy debates and decisionmaking, and to reallocate society's resources, environmental justice activism can ill afford an agenda driven solely by health impacts. Mortality and morbidity rates associated with causes that do not readily prompt outrage present significant obstacles to potential organizers.

Hazards perceived to be imposed on residents by firms—especially by ones viewed as community intruders—or by governmental actors suspected of being distant, unaccountable, or racist are more suitable for this purpose. Under such circumstances, anger and suspicion easily overwhelm risk and health as driving forces. Hazards linked strongly to individual behavior (such as smoking and excessive alcohol consumption) generally have far larger implications for personal and collective health but do not easily resonate politically. Telling neighborhood residents that an unfamiliar and unwanted company is fouling the local air or water, and perhaps threatening their children, can set the stage for effective community protest even when the actual health risks at stake are negligible. But reminding residents that they consume too many calories, or the wrong kinds of food, is likely to appear intrusive, insensitive, or simply beside the point.

Once their underlying democratizing aims are clearly understood it is not hard to make sense of the insistent emphasis by environmental justice activists and by grassroots environmentalists generally on relatively unlikely or weakly documented—but nevertheless profoundly fear-inducing—hazards, such as dioxin and Superfund sites. This democratizing imperative accounts for the deference regularly accorded intuitive (as opposed to scientific) perceptions of risk, as illustrated by the enduring folk myth of a so-called cancer alley in Louisiana (see below). Anemic mobilizing capacity (that is, low usefulness for generating collective outrage) helps explain why many well-established health hazards, including tobacco use, find no place in the litany of environmental justice concerns.

The political imperatives of the movement also explain why environmental justice lacks substantive health priorities. Real priorities would mean downgrading the concerns of at least some movement constituents, creating the great likelihood of conflict. Thomas Lambert and Christopher Boerner observe that although "environmental justice advocates often suggest creating various offices, councils, and task forces, they rarely detail how these entities should influence the pollution allocation process. Instead, they primarily advance general concepts of equality, not wishing to endanger their coalition by specifying the precise methods of achieving 'justice,' 'fairness,' or 'equity.'"[2] The egalitarian position that everyone should be heard and that no one should suffer maintains movement harmony, but at the cost of focus.

Two Approaches to Health

It is useful to highlight two contrasting (though not contradictory) emphases in government public health activity. For present purposes only—with the caveat that this necessarily makeshift terminology ought not be misconstrued—let us label them *regulatory* and *epidemiologic*.[3] A regulatory emphasis begins with potential hazards—mainly industrial products and processes—and asks: What risks might these pose to human health? Its tools include animal and human studies (toxicity tests, clinical trials, and epidemiologic studies) and mathematical risk models. Instead of focusing on citizen behavior, regulation concentrates mainly on the activities of firms that produce, distribute, or dispose of potentially dangerous material.

This approach may involve premarket approval by a regulatory body such as the Food and Drug Administration, which is charged with assessing risks and benefits of various drugs, cosmetics, and medical devices. In a similar vein the Toxic Substances Control Act (TSCA) requires that manufacturers notify the Environmental Protection Agency (EPA) before producing new chemical compounds. Such regulation of drugs, devices, and chemicals reflects an understandable desire to prevent new sources of harm instead of merely responding to them after they are manifest. TSCA supporter, Senator John Tunney (D-California), expected that the law's premarket screening system would "assure that we no longer have to wait for a body count or serious health damage to generate controls over hazardous chemicals."[4]

Regulation may also attach conditions to product use or result in the withdrawal of a product altogether. Beyond focusing on a product itself, regulation may also address the way it is made and any "externalities" (spillovers) generated. The general intention is to protect workers and the larger citizenry from various noxious effects to the extent deemed possible or feasible in light of applicable constraints (budgetary limits, income losses, and so on). Regulatory statutes vary widely in the extent to which they instruct agencies to balance risk against other concerns.[5]

A common hurdle faced by regulators is uncertainty regarding the nature and likelihood of the effects they wish to protect against. Regulation seeks to clarify, if possible, doses associated with specific toxic effects, but these are often not easily determined. Some substances might adversely affect certain groups in the population (that is, workers, children, or the elderly) more than the average citizen. Such enhanced vulnerability can be difficult for regulators to gauge using the limited data supplied by applicant firms or the available stock of scientific knowledge.

On the other hand, an epidemiologic approach does one of two things. It may begin with effects (that is, with the incidence of disease and premature death in a population) and then search for and address causes. Alternatively, it may focus on common behaviors or exposures and follow these across time to ascertain health outcomes.[6] The sudden appearance of discrete symptoms in a population—an "outbreak"—probably indicates the recurrence of a long familiar ailment, but it might in rare instances herald the recognition of some previously unknown problem (especially when closely associated in novel ways with characteristics such as location, age, gender, and various behaviors).[7] Of far greater significance to public health than novel outbreaks, however, are ongoing rates of continually important ailments such as coronary heart disease, stroke, hypertension, diabetes, asthma, and, of course, cancer. Although it originated as a new and frightening epidemic, Acquired Immune Deficiency Syndrome (AIDS), to the dismay of AIDS activists, is becoming similarly "normalized."

An epidemiologic analysis may often point to the role of individual behavior in causing and preventing harm. One can regulate, in painstaking detail, the design of automobiles and roads only to find that large numbers of persons continue to die or sustain preventable injury because they fail, in all-too-familiar ways, to drive with due care. An epidemiologic perspective also more naturally directs attention to all sources of harm, not just to regulated activities.

Epidemiologic analysis can often create a foundation for understanding, but the answers it provides may, for various reasons, prove unsatisfying. An array of uncertainties and confounding factors bedevil efforts to discern disease causation, especially where general environmental factors, rather than specific microbes or behaviors, are the suspected culprits.[8] Moreover, some persons (not all of them economic stakeholders) may be predisposed to distrust the results of analysis. As government officials have repeatedly found, grassroots victim organizations and their organizers often become deeply committed to the belief that perceived harms stem from proximate environmental toxins.[9] Attempted reassurances to the contrary may simply deepen existing mistrust. This is probably the clearest political lesson of the Love Canal and Agent Orange episodes in the recent past, and of the continuing imbroglio over Gulf War syndrome.[10]

For environmental justice to contribute measurably to public health in low-income and minority communities, it would almost certainly have to stress an epidemiologic perspective (even in connection with regulatory matters) to a far greater extent than is currently the case. Activism would have to begin with effects and then support honest, analytically defensible assessments of causal factors. But given the overriding concern with citizen mobilization and participation, the continuing focus on citizen fears and frustrations, and the strong incentives for those persons engaged in this activity to continue it, any such shift in perspective would be difficult to achieve.

True and False Alarms

Pollutants and chemical exposures can adversely affect human health. This is especially likely in occupational settings, where exposures are often orders of magnitude higher than in residential neighborhoods or the general environment. In the 1970s, for example, it was found that workers at a California pesticide plant had been rendered sterile as a result of heavy exposure to dibromochloropropane.[11] In the same decade occupational exposures to vinyl chloride were recognized as causing angiosarcoma, and kepone was found to cause both neurotoxicity and infertility.[12]

One of the most significant exposure risks for workers remains lead, a substance that has captured considerable attention in the environmental justice context (see below). A 1995 report by the federal Centers for Disease Control and Prevention (CDC) observed that "in the United States, an estimated 95 percent of elevated blood lead levels (BLLs) in adults are attributable to occupational exposure" especially among workers in the construction trades.[13] Such exposure can induce a variety of adverse effects, and one of the national health objectives for the year 2000 is to eliminate BLLs above 25 micrograms per deciliter in the blood of American workers.[14]

Accidents may also expose workers, and communities surrounding industrial facilities, to large doses of a contaminant. The most deadly incident of this sort in modern times is the December 1984 accidental release of methyl isocyanate in Bhopal, India, which killed 2,000 persons and injured thousands more.[15] Not long thereafter, a much less serious release of the same chemical at a Union Carbide plant in West Virginia led 130 persons to seek emergency treatment.[16] In another well-publicized incident in July 1976, an explosion at a chemical plant near Seveso, Italy, exposed residents to large quantities of the most toxic variant of dioxin—perhaps the most notorious and widely feared industrial by-product known to the general public.[17] A severe skin disease called chloracne developed in a number of persons exposed.

Ambient air pollutants may also affect human health adversely. For example, during national debate on a pending (and highly controversial) EPA standard for ozone, Lester Lave summarized what is known of ozone's health effects:

In the past decade, scientists have made considerable progress in understanding both the photochemistry of urban smog and the effects on people and plants. Ozone damages plants and obscures visibility. It is a respiratory irritant that can stop athletes from achieving peak performance or cause pain when people doing strenuous work breathe deeply. It can trigger asthma attacks. While there is a link between high ozone and hospital admissions and physician visits, in general the effects of ozone are reversible, disappearing within a few hours or days.[18]

Nevertheless, fear of environmentally induced disease vastly outstrips the extent of verifiable disease causation. Where infectious disease is concerned, clusters of illnesses are regularly a harbinger of a serious (if generally limited and manageable) problem amenable to previously successful intervention strategies.[19] Matters are quite different for noninfectious hazards, however, about which the CDC has advised:

> The reported experience of health agencies [in responding to clusters of noninfectious disease] confirms . . . that major associations between exposures and outcomes are rare. Minnesota, for example, has reported results from over 500 investigations of clusters, six of which were full-scale investigations. In one instance, in an occupational setting, an important public health outcome concerning cancer was documented. Missouri and Wisconsin have reported similar experiences: large numbers of requests for investigations have been received, but only an occasional in-depth evaluation is warranted. CDC has been consulted in over 100 such investigations, and again, major associations between exposures and outcomes have been rare.
>
> . . . The unofficial consensus among workers in public health is that most reports of clusters do not lead to a meaningful outcome. Often, a "case" is not clearly defined, and the "cluster" is, in fact, a mixture of different syndromes. Frequently, no exposure or potential cause is obvious, and—to make the investigation even more difficult—there are many possible causes. For example, an inactive toxic waste site may contain hundreds of chemicals. An investigation at the site may indicate no immediate or obvious connection between exposure and disease, and considerable manipulation may be required to demonstrate a statistically significant excess. Finally, the biologic consequences and public health impact often are not clear.[20]

Though it implied a skeptical stance toward clusters, the CDC was careful not to suggest that no real illnesses occur in such episodes. Instead, both the CDC and the American Public Health Association note that it is generally difficult to identify a scientifically meaningful aggregation of cases, much less that the apparent cluster has an identifiable cause.[21] This perspective helps set the stage for significant conflict between citizens and public health experts. Obviously aware of how high-handed and insensitive a health agency may appear to citizens whose concerns are too casually dismissed, the CDC counsels careful attention to "community relations."[22] Where a nascent environmental justice issue is concerned, such advice is even more appropriate, though this ought never mean acknowledging as certain something that cannot be demonstrated.

Cancer

When it comes to probably the gravest public health fear of all, human cancer, causal demonstration is especially uncertain. "Cancer" is dozens of different diseases, with typically long latency periods. Cancers of one kind or another affect every organ system, and they are common, causing about 20 percent of all deaths in America. While much attention has been focused on the few agents known to cause cancer—smoking, asbestos, ionizing radiation, sunlight, and some industrial chemicals—the causes of most cancers are unknown. In very few cases, and most of these involve smoking or asbestos, is a physician able to look at a patient and say with any certainty what caused the disease. Moreover most scientists agree both that cancer rates are not increasing (indeed, cancer mortality rates are declining) and that little of the cancer seen today is attributable to pollution.[23] A widely cited 1981 assessment by epidemiologists Richard Doll and Richard Peto concluded that only about 2 percent of cancer mortality derived from pollution (an estimate subjected to numerous criticisms).[24] On the other hand, every reputable authority and organization active in cancer policy and prevention incessantly refers to tobacco use as "the leading preventable cause of death in the United States," with lung cancer at the top of the list of preventable tobacco-related diseases.[25]

Even if one accepts that a very low number of cancer deaths can be attributed to pollution overall, it is still possible that pollution results in a disproportionate number of such deaths among minority or low-income persons. This would presumably be the case if such persons were disproportionately exposed to carcinogenic pollutants. This is possibly true in some places or for some substances, but it is unclear which such exposures (workplaces aside) are most usefully addressed for purposes of cancer prevention. Empirical work in the environmental justice literature is not helpful on this point as it relies on fairly crude proximity indicators that reveal nothing about actual exposure or carcinogenic potential. (Consider that everyone riding in an automobile is "exposed" to its possibly lethal supply of gasoline in the same sense.)

Our still limited understanding of cancer suggests that effective behavior modification will serve prevention far better than pollution controls. The obvious behavioral target is tobacco use. Health survey data indicate that "for certain population groups, particularly American Indians/Alaska Natives, blue collar workers, and military personnel, the rates of smoking prevalence are considerably higher than those for the population as a whole."[26] In analyzing 1987–91 data from the Behavioral Risk Factor Surveillance System, the CDC found that smoking prevalence was 33.4 percent among American Indian and Alaskan Native men and 26.6 percent for women. The percentages for whites were 25.7 and 23.0, respectively.[27] Moreover, while smoking prevalence declined with increasing income and education among whites, the rate of smoking was more than twice as high (37.5 percent) among college-educated American Indian and Alaskan Native men as among whites in the same category (14.6 percent).[28] The 1994 National Health Interview Survey found that 28 percent of white men smoked, while 33.9 percent and 53.7 percent of black and American Indian/Alaskan Native men, respectively, did.[29] While 24.1 percent of persons at or above the poverty line were current cigarette smokers, 34.7 percent of persons below were.[30] Obviously, to the extent that the disproportionate propensity to smoke is addressed successfully, so is the cancer risk (other things being equal).

While public health authorities and official data sources highlight dramatic differences in observable (and preventable) carcinogenic behavior, environmental justice has instead pursued the chimera of Louisiana's "cancer alley." The term refers to the roughly eighty-five-mile industrial corridor stretching from Baton Rouge to New Orleans, said to be home to one-quarter of the nation's petrochemical production.[31] The area is also home to many residents, including a large minority population, who have been convinced for years that living in the area carries with it significant additional cancer risk.

That citizen fear has found expression in environmental justice advocacy. In March 1993 testimony before a congressional subcommittee Pat Bryant of the Gulf Coast Tenants Association castigated the area as dangerous to the health of residents:

> "Cancer Alley" . . . remains one of the most poisoned areas anyplace. One hundred and thirty-eight petro-chemical facilities have made home in large plantations, most of the time as close as possible to African-American communities. . . .
>
> Despite denials of petro-chemical industry financed studies, we know that cancer incidence in this corridor is higher than the national average. Cancer is so commonplace in "Cancer Alley" that almost every family is touched.
>
> Roughly 2 billion pounds of poisons . . . known to cause cancer and mutagenics [sic], are dumped into the air, pumped in the land and water yearly in "Cancer Alley." This area has become a zone of national sacrifice. This is genocide at its finest, and is a national disgrace.[32]

It is not surprising that black Louisianans are seeing a lot of cancer since everyone else is, too. As science writer Michael Fumento observes: "one fourth of us will contract cancer and one fifth of us will die of it. Indeed, as the population ages and fewer and fewer people die of other causes, more and more will die of cancer."[33]

But have black Louisianans been seeing more cancer than other Americans? In 1990 the respective cancer incidence rates among blacks and whites nationally were 423 and 393 (per 100,000), a gap that experts suspect reflects some combination of differences in behavior and health care access.[34] In the 1970s some studies suggested an association between lung cancer incidence and the percentage of a population employed in or living near certain industries or in urban areas.[35] But these studies often failed to take smoking into account and they have not withstood scrutiny in the Louisiana case. The current scientific consensus is that behavioral and some occupational factors have been associated with cancer incidence in Louisiana, but that there is no overall "cancer epidemic" in that state or in the so-called cancer alley.[36] In fact, blacks in south Louisiana appeared to have had fewer cases of cancer than the national average during the 1983–87 period covered by the most careful study to date.[37] Although cancer incidence among blacks may have been low, mortality rates were excessive when compared with the nation as a whole, perhaps indicating that poor health care was a factor in the cancer burden among area residents.

Local environmental justice advocates and the larger grassroots environmental movement (notably Greenpeace and the Citizens Clearinghouse for Hazardous Waste) have made much of yet another alleged cancer threat: dioxin.[38] A by-product of certain industrial processes, especially herbicide production, there are seventy-five known varieties of dioxin. One of these—2,3,7,8-tetrachlorodibenzo-p-dioxin (TCDD)—is regarded as the most toxic and is often described in the media and by environmental advocacy groups as "the most deadly (or carcinogenic) chemical created by man."[39] Dioxin exposure is apparently universal among humans and "among North Americans generally, the concentration of dioxin in body fat ranges from nondetectable levels to 20 parts per trillion."[40]

This fearsome image is rooted not in identified human cancers but in animal studies and in three widely publicized (and well documented) health scares. In animal tests, dioxin is, indeed, the most potent carcinogen ever tested, but the tested doses are thousands of times higher than environmental exposures. The health scares have included: (1) the 1979 crisis at Love Canal that placed hazardous waste on the national political agenda; (2) the claim by some Vietnam veterans that exposure to Agent Orange, an herbicide containing TCDD, led to various adverse health consequences; and (3) the infamous Times Beach, Missouri, episode in which the spraying of a community's roads with contaminated waste oil happened to precede a disastrous flood. Many analysts now regard the health impacts at issue in each of these episodes to have been considerably exaggerated.[41]

The only well established (that is, undisputed) human health effect of TCDD exposure remains chloracne. The EPA has been unable to assess whether dioxin is a human carcinogen at low (nonoccupational) doses, but a working group of twenty-five scientists meeting at the International Agency for Research on Cancer (IARC) in Lyon, France, in February 1997 concluded that TCDD slightly increased "the overall risk of lung cancer and of all cancers combined . . . in the most highly exposed workers."[42] The working group's conclusions were based less on the limited epidemiologic evidence available than on animal data and on presumed similarities between animals and humans, a common but extremely controversial risk assessment approach.[43]

Environmental Hormones

The various dioxins and other "dioxin-like" compounds (including some polychlorinated biphenyls, or PCBs) have recently been targeted by some scientists and environmentalists on somewhat different grounds: that such man-made chemicals, individually and in combination, may cause subtle but ultimately tragic reproductive consequences as "hormone disrupters" in both animals and humans. The spring of 1996 witnessed the release of *Our Stolen Future*, a well-promoted volume (containing a foreword by Vice President Al Gore) that argued for such a possibility.[44] There followed sharp criticism that the book had been cleverly packaged to alarm and mislead a credulous public, that its assertions of declining sperm counts and other effects were unsubstantiated, and that there was actually no justification for attacking synthetic hormones while ignoring the far more abundant stock of natural ones.[45] Shortly thereafter, researchers reported in the journal *Science* that mixtures of pesticides acted synergistically on estrogen receptors. These results suggested that combinations of pesticides at concentrations now permitted in the environment pose a danger to human and animal hormone systems. This finding generated press reports of a newly discovered set of possible "environmental estrogens."[46] But because neither the original experimenters nor others were able to duplicate these findings, the original report in *Science* was formally withdrawn by its authors the following year.[47] Regarding environmental hormone disrupters, more research is clearly warranted before major, and immensely costly, regulatory remedies are adopted.[48]

Though the scientific jury is still out, and likely to remain so for a considerable time to come, environmental justice supporters have strongly advocated highlighting environmental hormones. In the view of grassroots environmentalists, the issue puts pressure where it belongs: on a governmental-corporate alliance responsible for poisoning communities and perhaps threatening human fertility. In March 1996, the same month that *Our Stolen Future* was published, a reported 600 activists gathered in solidarity at the Third Citizens' Conference on Dioxin and Other Synthetic Hormone Disrupters.[49]

Children and Farmworkers

If the empirical case for pollution-related cancers and disrupted hormones as environmental justice priorities remains questionable, two other issues rest on conspicuously firmer foundations: exposures of minority children to environmental lead and occupational exposure of the largely Latino farmworker population to agricultural chemicals. In both instances there are reasonable grounds for continuing concern. Possibly the most ironic and insidious effect of grassroots environmentalism's determination to make everything a priority is an inevitably diminished capacity for concentrating both funding and public attention on the far narrower range of targets that merit major effort.

Though neither ranks with tobacco use or alcohol abuse as a health problem, both childhood lead and farmworker chemical exposures deserve serious and sustained attention. But even these issues are subject to the uncertainty, controversy, and tradeoffs that often render health and safety policymaking far from simple. Moreover, the diligent compliance of individuals, not just business enterprises, is essential.

The EPA's 1992 environmental equity workgroup report noted "clear differences between racial groups in terms of disease and death" while admitting that there were "limited data to explain the environmental contribution to these differences."[50] Data that might reveal such associations were not being collected.

However, a single substance seemed to have avoided these bleak analytic prospects. "The notable exception," according to the report, "is lead poisoning: A significantly higher percentage of Black children compared to White children have unacceptably high blood lead levels."[51] This conclusion derived from a 1988 report by the Agency for Toxic Substances and Disease Registry (ATSDR) estimating that *more than two-thirds (68 percent) of urban black children with incomes below $6,000 had BLLs above 15 micrograms/deciliter.* The number of such children declined with rising incomes; 54 percent of urban black children in the $6,000–$15,000 range and 38 percent of those with incomes above $15,000 were estimated to have such BLLs. The respective estimates for urban white children in these income categories were 36 percent , 23 percent , and 12 percent.[52]

Even in the case of childhood lead, however, a number of uncertainties and disputed issues remain. As various studies have associated adverse effects, especially intellectual deficits, with lower childhood BLLs, the threshold level of concern promoted by CDC has been rapidly lowered. That official threshold has declined from 30 micrograms per deciliter in the period 1975–85, to 25 micrograms in 1985–91, to the current 10 micrograms.[53] One critic of federal lead policy observes that the current threshold of 10 micrograms would have been exceeded by "about 99 percent of the population" in 1960.[54]

At the time it issued the environmental equity report, the EPA was sure that low-income and minority children were more prone to elevated BLLs but unsure exactly what was causing them. The EPA believed that various past uses of lead were the source of the disproportionate elevations, with lead-based paint ranking as the "most significant" source, according to a high agency official.[55] Other primary sources included urban soil and dust and contaminated drinking water.

Copious research findings have been marshaled over the years to argue that lead adversely affects the intellectual capacities and behavior of many children (although some critics regard the risks of levels nearing 10 micrograms to be unproved or exaggerated).[56] This evidence of persisting victimization to young innocents (rather than to adults) of all backgrounds (not just minorities and the poor) has made the childhood lead issue politically attractive. Ironically, some environmental justice advocates manifest impatience with the issue, convinced that lead is only the tip of a large iceberg of pollution disproportionately affecting minority communities, yet suspicious that the establishment uses a focus on lead to escape responsibility for a far broader range of pollution hazards.

The lead issue has clearly proved amenable to politically feasible legislative interventions. As far back as 1972 Congress passed a Lead-Based Paint Poisoning and Prevention Act. Lead-based paint (which, when old and cracked, flakes off in small, sweet-tasting chips and dust that can be ingested by small children) was banned in 1978. Congress passed the Residential Lead Based Paint Hazard Reduction Act in 1992, and federal regulations published in 1996 require real estate sellers and landlords to disclose to buyers and renters of property any information about lead paint on the premises.[57]

The single most effective policy decision reducing national BLLs in recent years—ironically a decision largely devoid of group advocacy, racial or otherwise—was probably the accelerated phaseout of leaded gasoline by the EPA announced in 1985. The phaseout stemmed from a fortunate confluence of policy analysis (showing significant public health benefits), policy vision (by senior EPA officials), and politics (because the Reagan administration was anxious to deflect criticism of its environmental record).[58] Whatever its origins, the phaseout has yielded a dramatic reduction in airborne lead. By 1995 the United States and Canada accounted for nearly half (44 percent) of gasoline consumption but only 1.2 percent of world lead emissions.[59]

At present further reduction in lead exposure and ingestion among children of all races seems to require mainly diligent attention to personal hygiene and monitoring of BLLs in children likely to be exposed. National reductions in airborne lead emissions have undoubtedly benefited urban minority children the most, since they were disproportionately likely to show high BLLs. But "de-leading" of the nation's entire housing stock is probably impractical on economic grounds. Strong evidence of disproportionate adverse impact on low income and minority children makes lead poisoning a reasonable environmental justice priority. But it is an area where personal compliance, enduring uncertainties (including possibly flawed research), and broader tradeoffs remain inescapable.[60]

The case for highlighting farmworker chemical exposures is also strong, even though the issue's empirical foundation is less sturdy and the tradeoffs involved arguably more daunting. The combination of migratory farmwork and chemical use (including the potent insecticides, fungicides, and rodenticides enumerated in the title of the relevant federal regulatory statute) helps to produce an abundant—and therefore reasonably-priced—national food supply.[61] Farmworker activists like NEJAC member Baldemar Velasquez, head of the Farm Labor Organizing Committee, may fundamentally oppose agricultural chemicals in principle but realize that the interests of growers and consumers, and the realities of modern agribusiness, will probably dictate continued use of chemicals for years to come. Moreover, farmworker advocates obviously do not want to destabilize the economic underpinnings of the already precarious livelihoods of their constituents. Velasquez has spoken publicly of the fundamental stake that farmworkers have in "a healthy, vibrant industry."[62]

Persons concerned about long-term chemical risks to farmworkers confront severe information gaps. In a contribution to the volume *Race and the Incidence of Environmental Hazards*, Ivette Perfecto observes:

> Documenting the link between pesticides and health is difficult because most pesticide illnesses go untreated. In 1976, farm worker surveys in California led state officials to estimate that only a small fraction, perhaps only one or two percent, of pesticide-induced illnesses of field workers was being reported. . . .
>
> Chronic health effects related to pesticide exposure are largely unknown due to the lack of attention from the research community, the lack of a record keeping method that would provide the necessary information to document pesticide exposure, and the long period of clinical latency for some of the effects. . . .[63]

Despite uncertainty about health effects, the occupational context is inherently problematic enough to warrant sustained caution and regulatory attention. It is a setting where powerful chemicals are mixed and applied. Workers must function in recently treated areas and handle recently treated produce. In many circumstances, workers themselves must don personal protective equipment, with both farmworkers and growers abiding by guidelines regarding when and where it is safe to work.

The EPA has struggled to define exactly what is permissible and prohibited in the farm chemical field, with major rules taking effect in 1992 and 1995.[64] As one should expect, the agency's challenge stems from the variety of chemicals, products, tasks, and interests involved and an overall context of uncertainty. Regulations needed to be stringent enough to protect workers but sufficiently flexible to avoid unduly burdening growers. In May 1995, for example, after pleas from the agricultural community, the EPA granted an administrative exception to its 1992 Worker Protection Standard by allowing workers "to perform necessary irrigation activities, which if delayed could cause significant economic loss, and that result in minimal contact with pesticide-treated surfaces," for up to eight of any twenty-four hours during a restricted-entry interval.[65]

Despite the EPA's efforts, farmworker protection remains a contentious and uneven enterprise. The EPA has sought to emphasize worker information and training, but advocate Baldemar Velasquez complained to a representative from the EPA's pesticide program during a May 1996 NEJAC meeting that "you give [farmworkers] information but you don't give them the ability to do anything about the abuses," a complaint doubtless anchored, ultimately, in the political clout enjoyed by growers. Meanwhile, an EPA representative at the meeting pointed to an array of difficulties: getting farmworkers to attend outreach and training meetings, wide variation in compliance effort among states and growers, lingering public confusion between the roles of the EPA and the Occupational Safety and Health Administration in protecting farmworkers, and grower misperceptions of the level of stringency the EPA was actually demanding.[66]

Despite such difficulties, farmworker protection remains easily defensible as an environmental justice health priority. If nothing else, the concentrated exposures involved (attested to by instances of acute chemical poisoning) indicate that potentially serious risks are present. The case for taking special precautions against victimization is further bolstered because the disproportionately Latino farmworker constituency consists overwhelmingly of persons of modest incomes and limited education, and includes many persons with little or no command of English.

Asthma and Indoor Air Pollution

Asthma, another problem affecting African Americans disproportionately, highlights an epidemiologic perspective. A disorder marked by "paroxysmal dyspnea" (that is, recurring spasms of breathing difficulty), asthma affects an estimated 14 million persons in the United States.[67] According to the American Lung Association, African Americans account for 22.1 percent of asthma-related deaths.[68] The disease appears disproportionately prevalent among inner-city residents, although it is unclear why.[69] Recent research implicates cockroach allergen in childhood asthma.[70] More generally, house-dust mites, animal dander, and mold appear causally related to asthma.

Because minorities reside disproportionately in urban areas (which inevitably have the greatest difficulty achieving attainment with national clean air goals), and because ambient air pollution may play a role in triggering asthma attacks and other breathing problems, controls on airborne emissions might appear justified on environmental justice grounds. Environmental justice enthusiasts refer repeatedly to various air pollution studies, dating as far back as a 1971 report by the Council on Environmental Quality, in support of the more general claim that minorities face greater exposure burdens.[71] But it has proven politically impossible to racialize the issue of urban air pollution, a problem that affects many affluent and nonminority citizens and that offers no dramatic solutions (such as restricted industrial development or automobile use) that would not unduly burden both minority and nonminority city dwellers. Suspicion that greater air pollution exposure might combine with other disproportionate environmental burdens to yield significantly more adverse health effects among people of color is mere speculation.

The indoor environment appears a far more promising focus of asthma prevention and management (and of efforts to prevent acute poisoning unrelated to asthma) than ambient pollution levels. Reducing exposure to various known or suspected allergens, and enabling individuals to prevent and treat acute attacks, are undoubtedly where public policy for asthma must aim, for blacks and whites alike.

Intuition and Health

Industrial pollution looms far larger in the minds of citizens than in the opinion of experts as a danger to human health, an oft-noted divergence of perspectives.[72] Observers have stressed various explanations for the difference and for the persistent conflict and dissatisfaction thereby generated. Howard Margolis sorts these theories into three categories: ideology, trust, and rival rationalities. As Margolis explains:

> Theory 1 is that these expert/lay conflicts are only in form about risk. What in fact (on this view) is driving matters are deeper conflicts about power and responsibility, about human obligations to other humans and to nature, and hence about what ends public policy is going to serve. In short, the controversy is about *ideology*, not risk. Theory 2, on the other hand, allows the controversy to be about just what the experts think it is about, but the problem lies in a loss of *trust* by the public in the institutions that seek to assure it that danger is under control. Theory 3, finally, turns on the idea . . . that what the expert sees as risk is not the same thing as what the public sees. The expert is concerned with some quantitative measure, such as expected fatalities. But the public is concerned with a far broader sense of danger that includes many dimensions beyond expected fatalities. So of course expert and lay judgment may diverge. I will call this last the *rival rationalities view*.[73]

Margolis deems each theory unsatisfying, essentially assessing each as explaining too little or too much.[74] Margolis constructs a useful alternative argument around the role of human intuition in governing citizen perceptions of risk. Drawing on findings in social psychology, Margolis argues that "what we are seeing [in persistent citizen divergence from expert judgment about risk] is the unconscious cuing of habits of mind" (that is, intuition).[75] The problem, as Margolis explains, is that "in contexts out of the range of familiar experience . . . ordinarily effective cognitive processes can lead to confident intuitions that eventually come to look plainly wrong."[76]

Part of what can lead us astray is that we become *sensitized* to some sources of risk (such as dioxin, with its perverse Vietnam War association) but *habituated* to others (such as aflatoxin, a far more demonstrably significant human carcinogen—encountered in peanut butter—that few citizens ever hear of).[77] Moreover, for subtle or novel risks not readily identified with useful or pleasurable activities, it may be difficult to prompt in citizens a sense of "fungibility," that is, a recognition that dangers avoided lead to opportunities forgone.

Even though travel by auto and airplane is demonstrably risky, citizens are more prepared to weigh risks against benefits, and to rely on expert assessment regarding how the tradeoffs ought to be managed. This is not the case with environmental chemical exposures, which are too exotic to prompt fungibility, partly because the choice at stake can be made to appear to be between *zero* additional risk on the one hand and some inherently *unacceptable* (no matter how small) additional risk on the other.[78] Drawing on findings in social psychology research, Margolis observes that "the cases of sharp expert/lay conflicts of intuition are in fact usually cases where the statistical risks to an individual are very small—indeed, microscopic."[79]

A human tendency to reason intuitively rather than logically is pervasive. It is not associated with any particular ethnic group or income level. The illiterate and the Ivy Leaguer alike lie vulnerable to intuition's thrall, accounting for such widespread beliefs as the waxing and waning of pain according to changes in the weather or the value of astrology for predicting human personalities.[80] "If you look at people as intuitive scientists," observes social psychologist Amos Tversky, "you find that we are very good at pattern generation, we are very good at generating hypotheses. It's just that we are not very good at all at actually testing hypotheses," because the rigorous testing and rejection of hypotheses contradicts the intuitive impulse.[81]

Although members of all groups manifest the same intuitive limitations, one may reasonably suggest that racial or ethnic identity, in tandem with proximity to something both unfamiliar and undesirable, can trigger a particularly tenacious version of intuitive risk perception. When citizens reside in a given location, and are aware of one another as racially or ethnically distinctive, it is not difficult to incline them to view that distinctiveness as profoundly causal, particularly if those citizens have good reason historically to suspect that bad things will befall them because of their distinctiveness. If those citizens note some especially common problem in their midst for which there is no readily apparent cause or cure (such as cancer), it is not surprising that they would grope for an explanation of this apparent anomaly by reference to something nearby that does not prompt fungibility—a dump, an incinerator, or some other facility. Nor is it to be wondered why they might reflexively think the worst of anyone proposing to place such a facility nearby. On the other hand, where risk stems from something familiar or useful, perhaps even cherished, negative effects may be hard to impute, no matter how well-founded expert concerns are.

Consider the black residents of the Escambia neighborhood of Pensacola, Florida, who decided that a nearby Superfund site— dubbed "Mount Dioxin" by the residents—was causing adverse health effects. They not only demanded federally subsidized relocation but refused to cooperate with official efforts to assess residents' health, apparently convinced that such an assessment would yield biased (and unfavorable) results. Residents "knew" there was a connection between the site and their sicknesses, and that both had something to do with their race. They became determined not to take no for an answer (and ultimately were successful).[82]

At the same time Escambia residents pressed their cause before the EPA, Mexican health officials battled citizen indifference to a clear, but unthreatening, hazard. Studies had demonstrated dangerously high BLLs among Mexican potter clans due to their use of lead glazing, but the potters were inclined to scoff at the idea that they were vulnerable to lead poisoning. "When I was a baby, my mother gave me chamomile tea from cups like the ones we make," said one. "My wife gave our babies tea from those cups. My son does well in primary school. My daughter is a whiz—she plays the piano!" Asked another: "How could we make such beautiful pottery if we were dull and sick?"[83]

Closer to home, many Afro-Caribbean and Latino New Yorkers have regularly exposed themselves and their loved ones to a dangerous poison through the ritualistic and residential use of mercury, to which some persons ascribe mystical protective or curative powers.[84] Sold in a variety of containers and often without appropriate warning labels by neighborhood shops known as botanicas, metallic mercury may well be associated with significant adverse effects in homes where it is burned, sprinkled, or otherwise distributed to encourage good fortune. Yet any harm resulting from these practices is not only self-inflicted but also culturally sanctioned. Moreover, no readily apparent epidemic of mercury-related disease has generated the overtly "visible victims" often necessary to motivate aggressive action on the part of already overburdened public health officials.[85] Attempts to call attention to the risks involved have regularly met indifference and sometimes even outright hostility.[86]

Such is the power of human intuition. Policymakers fail, at their peril, to take this dimension of the risk management challenge into account. Persons who would either counsel policymakers or mobilize residents should realize that encouraging and drawing strength from citizen intuitions about risk may divert attention from relatively serious risks to far less significant ones. Communities already disproportionately beset by an array of problems may be particularly victimized by such diversions.

Beyond Health

One obvious qualification to the preceding line of argument is that environmental protection is not intended only to safeguard human health. Recognizing the problems of casting environmental justice in strict health terms, an EPA political appointee suggests that a far more inclusive concept than health—quality of life—better describes the citizen aspirations at work. Surely this official has a point, one long accepted both in his agency and among states that have pursued comparative risk projects embracing substantial citizen involvement.[87]

What animates a community like Chester, Pennsylvania, where residents have battled a concentration of facility sitings, is not a clear indication that higher rates of disease and death are linked to pollution. Rather, the community simply appears to have been bombarded by much that is malodorous and otherwise painful or distasteful. An economically troubled area since the departure of many better-paying factory jobs, Chester has had more than its share of general unpleasantness, and residents understandably want some of its more egregious manifestations reduced or eliminated. In places like Chester, intuitively grounded health anxieties can help provide leverage for community mobilizing that is actually grounded in quality-of-life concerns and a sense of general unfairness. Partly because of this, and partly because mere evidence to the contrary (with its inevitable ambiguities and gaps) is simply overmatched in contests with popular intuition, science or health data alone, no matter how capably pursued or patiently explained, should not be expected to constitute an acceptable response to citizen fears. Instead, officials may sometimes be better off combating popular intuitions about minor risks with an alternative intuition focused on the possible costs *to citizens* associated with reducing such risks to zero.

5

OPPORTUNITY

ALONG WITH greater community involvement and reduced health risks, the enhancement of economic opportunity in low-income and minority locales has emerged as a central theme of environmental justice policy and political discourse. As this chapter suggests, constraints abound on this front, although a profound social equity problem is undeniable. Wealthier and better-educated citizens enjoy greater flexibility than poorer, less-educated ones, not only in shaping personal environments to their satisfaction but also in extracting material benefits from environmentalism and its myriad spin-offs. Better-off persons can be more selective in their residential and occupational choices, a latitude that facilitates avoidance of less desirable, and perhaps riskier, locations and jobs.[1] If individual skills, experience, and educational credentials (as well as the social networks tying people together) help one earn a living through environment-related activity, some persons and groups are bound to be better equipped than others. No government, especially if democratic and market-oriented, can eliminate such inequality. Having little money or education has severe consequences: a greatly restricted menu of life's amenities, some of them environmental. This is arguably the foundation of most environmental inequity.

One might conceivably mitigate inequality at the margins, in particular places, or among designated persons. Not every "free market" outcome need be accepted as inevitable, nor are all forms of inequality equally intractable. Social security is our most popular and successful antipoverty policy (although it is not usually described as such). By dispensing monthly benefit checks, the federal government effectively provides millions of elderly retirees a guaranteed minimum income. Martha Derthick's observation of social security in the 1970s remains valid today: "There is not the slightest evidence that the American people would like to do away with the program, nor can there be any doubt that the aged people of this country are better off because of it."[2]

More controversial, and markedly more uneven, have been attempts to support the incomes of working-age persons through stimulated economic development or through programs (such as remedial education, job training, job search assistance, and job readiness coaching) intended to raise the employment prospects of targeted beneficiaries. Because such policies require much more than simple check writing, often concentrate on persons and places that are troubled in severe and complicated ways, and often apply uncertain (and perhaps untested) methods, it is not surprising that they have proved far more problematic than social security.

Might creatively implemented environmental programs help alleviate economic inequality? To be plausible such efforts must at the very least avoid certain political landmines. In an era of pervasive fiscal constraint and vigorous challenges to the more rigid or aggressive forms of affirmative action, the effort should not be perceived either as costly or as fundamentally unfair. Since economic inequality, or lack of opportunity, is an underlying systemic grievance among environmental justice advocates, one might expect their support for extracting the maximum economic benefit from environmental programs. If such policies appear consistent with generating commercial opportunity, business may conceivably support them. Finally, such efforts must anticipate and address community fears of exploitation; anxiety that the resulting jobs might promote lax enforcement or harmful chemical exposures is a common reservation expressed by residents and activists. But assuming that all these hurdles have been cleared, opportunity as an environmental justice theme should have a reasonably sound political foundation. Not surprisingly Clinton administration efforts on this front strive to satisfy these conditions.

Although regulatory programs are not primarily intended to serve redistributive ends, the basic plausibility of such efforts hinges on the fact that environmental programs and policy decisions routinely trigger expenditures of public and private funds, both directly and indirectly. Environmental programs both hire workers and cause workers to be hired to perform tasks related to hazard remediation and regulatory compliance. The wastewater treatment construction grants program of the Environmental Protection Agency (EPA) is a multibillion dollar public works subsidy, and billions more are spent on solid and hazardous waste management and remediation.[3] Environmental programs, and an enduring public enthusiasm for environmentalism, also sustain demand for legions of analysts—engineers, lawyers, academics, journalists, and various environmental health specialists. Having more persons of color among their ranks is clearly desirable. Some commentators propose that environmentalism can pay direct economic dividends because of global demand for "environment-friendly" products and processes.[4] Might there be a role for environmental justice in the pursuit of those benefits? In a different vein, as suggested below, environmental programs might themselves inadvertently impede investment and job creation; if so, thoughtful program reform might improve matters in communities of color as well as society as a whole. Given all these possibilities, it is no wonder that protest originating in a kind of racialized NIMBY (not in my back yard) advocacy and claims of disproportionate burden has broadened to include a search for creative ways to do something *for* people of color, instead of *to* them, under the more positive rubric of environmental justice.

Paths to Progress

In at least five ways environmental programs might, if only modestly, promote economic opportunity among people and communities of color. The most obvious and direct way is through employment and promotion of such persons within government—that is, through diversity efforts and affirmative action within the EPA and other federal or state agencies. To be sure, public sector employment has proved a primary pathway into the middle class for many African Americans. But with a grand total of only 18,000 positions in fiscal year 1996, even a major increase in the minority presence at the EPA would likely be barely perceptible in the overall employment picture, although similar effort by other agencies and levels of government may brighten it somewhat.

One could argue for diversity efforts on other grounds, however. Perhaps having more minority personnel inside environmental bureaucracies might advance the goal of democratic involvement by rendering those agencies more reliably accommodating to minority policy concerns, especially if some of those persons occupied key decisionmaking roles. On the other hand, the connection between attitudes and behavior in organizations is, at best, tenuous. Many factors besides racial solidarity (including professional socialization and constraints linked to statutes, resource levels, institutional history, lower-level enforcement discretion, political realities, and so on) condition the performance of officials of *any* race in government agencies.[5] During the first Clinton term both the head of EPA's hazardous waste program, assistant administrator Elliott P. Laws, and his deputy assistant administrator, Timothy Fields, were African Americans with a strong professed commitment to environmental justice. But this hardly meant that the Superfund program could be run with only environmental justice considerations in mind.

Remaining economic opportunity prospects lie mainly in the private sector. A second path to progress is employment in the context of environmental remediation; as noted above, cleaning up contaminated sites is a potentially rewarding business. As Clarice Gaylord, director of the EPA's Office of Environmental Equity, testified before Congress in 1993: "Our belief is that residents can be put to work to clean up their own communities, and that is a program we are testing."[6]

A third and related possibility is employment in facility construction after an environmental cleanup is completed. A contaminated site's subsequent use might generate local employment. Initially, such benefits might stem from installing a new economic entity, whether public or private, and its infrastructure.

This leads to a fourth, and perhaps the most intriguing, possibility: ongoing employment of nearby residents at whatever entity is completed and functioning. This is presumably where long-term jobs, perhaps even positions with potential for advancement, might arise.

A fifth and final possibility is that the government might offer, subsidize, or mandate training and credentialing that tie in specifically to the other four or to the broader array of labor market prospects. As elaborated below, such efforts are underway but must confront a rather disappointing (or difficult to interpret) record of earlier programs along with limited political support.[7]

Fields of Dreams

Ironically, the third and fourth pathways appear especially viable today largely because of a recognition that only relatively modest cleanups, if any, are necessary at many sites where development is desirable. Experience with Superfund and other environmental programs teaches that such efforts may inadvertently create harmful, if perhaps reducible, barriers to much desired local development. The Clinton administration envisions its brownfields redevelopment initiative, aimed at sites that may be mildly contaminated from previous industrial use, as serving the cause of environmental justice.

The brownfields problem of undeveloped or underutilized urban locations stems largely from the character of the Comprehensive Environmental Response, Compensation, and Liability Act (CERCLA, the statute creating Superfund) and the pervasive investment disincentives it inadvertently spawned. Hurriedly enacted by a lame-duck Democratic Congress in the waning days of the Carter administration, CERCLA codified liability among potentially responsible parties (PRPs) and established a $1.6 billion trust fund (later quintupled under the 1986 Superfund Amendments and Reauthorization Act). As Congress envisioned the Superfund program, responsible parties would pay for most cleanups, not the taxpayer. The fund would serve as both a first and a last resort. It would make prompt cleanups possible—"shovels first, lawyers later" it was said—and be available when no responsible party (or at least none with sufficiently deep pockets) could be found to pay for a cleanup.

Severe deficiencies in the Superfund program have been apparent for a long time, quite apart from the reluctant and scandal-plagued enforcement that prevailed in the early Reagan years.[8] Throughout the 1980s frustratingly few cleanups were completed, as PRPs feverishly sought to avoid liability, setting off an explosion of litigation.

Congress did not anticipate the debilitating economic taint that could adhere to any location in which the Superfund program showed even the slightest formal interest. Superfund liability concerns made manufacturers, developers, lenders, insurers, and others reluctant to invest in many locations. A 1990 federal district court decision in *United States v. Fleet Factors Corporation* made matters worse, holding that "a secured creditor could be liable under CERCLA if its involvement with a facility's management is 'sufficiently broad to support the inference that it could affect hazardous waste disposal decisions if it so chose,'" even if the creditor remained uninvolved in day-to-day facility operations.[9] A representative of the American Bankers Association testified to Congress that the broad standard of lender liability created by *Fleet Factors* "is sending shock waves through the lending community."[10]

Although contamination at a site might be mild, trivial, or even nonexistent—in the absence of exploratory sampling one cannot know for sure—the financial risk could easily seem prohibitive. Firms preferred to let potentially marketable properties lie fenced off and undisturbed, lest they rouse the sleeping giant of liability.

For the same reason, a bank might even avoid foreclosing on a property. In urban areas, where mildly contaminated sites abound, a dread of liability impeded otherwise viable and much desired development.[11] Merely being listed on EPA's Comprehensive Environmental Response, Compensation, and Liabilities Information System (CERCLIS) inventory of more than 35,000 sites (an indicator of possible future federal action) could be enough to deter interest in development. Moreover, these "brownfields" (as they came to be called) were not only a direct environmental and economic burden. There were indirect effects as well, since the development they could displace might threaten relatively undisturbed suburban "greenfields" that posed fewer assessment burdens and no cleanup headaches. Small wonder that by the mid-1990s the U.S. Conference of Mayors ranked brownfields revitalization as its top environmental policy priority, with environmentalists (anxious to protect greenfields) very inclined to sympathize.

Politically, brownfields redevelopment has broad appeal. Such sites are pervasive. Revitalization enlists both liberals anxious to help depressed areas or protect the environment along with enterprise-minded conservatives. It also provides potentially lucrative work for environmental consultants, contractors, and attorneys. The EPA came to believe that by cooperating aggressively with the states, and by offering relatively small amounts of funding as a planning and assessment catalyst, significant parcels of land could be reclaimed for productive use without endangering the public's health.

The Clinton EPA awarded the first brownfield pilot grant, $200,000, to Cuyahoga County (Cleveland) Ohio in November 1993.[12] Two more (Richmond, Virginia, and Bridgeport, Connecticut) followed in 1994 and fifteen more in July 1995. By mid-1998 the EPA boasted of having provided funding to "157 states, cities, towns, counties, and tribes" since fiscal year 1995.[13] The grants would, according to the EPA, "test redevelopment models, direct special efforts toward removing regulatory barriers without sacrificing protectiveness and facilitate coordinated public and private efforts at [all] levels [of government]." Federal funds would help bring together community groups, investors, lenders, developers, and other affected parties "to address the issue of assessing and cleaning up brownfields and returning them to appropriate and productive use."

Of course, the EPA could do more than offer funding. Shortly after announcing the Brownfields Action Agenda in January 1995, Administrator Carol Browner could boast that the agency had "archived" (that is, removed from active Superfund consideration) some 24,000 CERCLIS sites (the number would later rise to 27,000).[14] More important was the EPA's demonstrated commitment to clarify liability and to reassure states, lenders, prospective purchasers, innocent landowners, and others that in a wide range of circumstances the agency would have no interest in coming after them or in second-guessing decisions made at lower levels of government. In short, during Browner's tenure, the EPA has come to think of itself as being in partnership with the variety of stakeholders involved in brownfields redevelopment.

There is little doubt that brownfields redevelopment has yielded some visible successes already. Several have been described in considerable depth by the Northeast-Midwest Institute in an ongoing series of publications.[15] Whether in designated EPA brownfields pilots, or under the aegis of state voluntary cleanup programs blessed by the EPA, numerous sites have been or are being developed across the country. The institute's recent compilation of twenty brownfield case studies indicates that many sites have yielded or can be expected to attract jobs, sometimes in significant numbers, as well as an enhanced tax base. Two Minnesota sites, for example— one a business park, the other a shopping mall—are expected to generate 350 and 1,700 jobs respectively.

Only in time can analysis address the obvious outcome questions: Do brownfields projects overall, and over the long run, increase net employment and local economic vitality by a lot, a little, or not at all? Will brownfields redevelopment projects sometimes merely bleed jobs away from other locales? What specific kinds of development will actually turn out to be most beneficial to communities?

Assuming that anyone poses such questions, they will not be answerable for years to come.

The EPA's Office of Solid Waste and Emergency Response has had to cultivate activist and community support for its brownfields program, addressing early suspicions that the initiative was excessively "top-down" and might lead to less-than-ideal land uses.[16] Given the substantial number of minority and disadvantaged persons in many areas coveting revitalization, the relative ease of embracing "community involvement" as a redevelopment theme, and the prospect that much-needed jobs will result, it is not surprising that brownfields and environmental justice are sometimes discussed as if a meshing of the two were natural.

It is not necessarily natural at all. The concentrated employment need of a particular population subgroup is implausible as a primary incentive for the overwhelming majority of redevelopment projects. Many sites and jobs may simply not be realistically accessible for many poor, unemployed, or underemployed persons. Furthermore, the lists of "key players" identified in the emerging case study literature provide little reason to think that producing jobs for unemployed persons will be a driving factor. The impetus for projects will far more likely be perceived matches between the interests of existing economic entities and the opportunities presented to them by development prospects at specific locations. These entities will include manufacturers, service establishments, real estate interests, and nonprofit corporations. Among firms anxious to grow, and to generate employment opportunity as a by-product, it is clearly implausible to imagine that a desire to rescue the so-called hard-core unemployed would be a foremost consideration. The brownfields redevelopment rationale argues merely that government ought to help localities make the most of their assets, at the very least by removing unnecessary barriers where possible. Thus brownfields revitalization is conceptually too modest to constitute a serious antipoverty effort.

This is not to say that brownfields redevelopment projects will not produce jobs for environmental justice constituencies. Some projects doubtless will. Rather, the point here is that such revitalization may be hard pressed to dependably produce employment gains for the disadvantaged in part because doing so will be hard to incorporate and sustain as a project focus, even in the relatively small number of instances when a motivated and resourceful community-based organization (CBO) happens to be on the scene to help do so. Nurtured by foundation support, CBOs, and especially community development corporations (CDCs), have scored successes in neighborhood redevelopment, especially in the provision of housing.[17] But theirs appears likely to be a subordinate role, at best, in most brownfields projects.

Some would argue that a limited reliance on certain kinds of CBO activity would be all to the good. Harvard economist Michael E. Porter believes that the economic distress facing America's inner cities is largely a failure to keep government obstructionism and local activist meddling at bay while successfully enticing "private, for-profit initiatives and investments based on economic self-interest and genuine competitive advantage."[18] Porter's argument has, in turn, been challenged as ill-informed and even fanciful on a number of counts.[19] The EPA/Housing and Urban Development (HUD) program is premised on the widely accepted view that government, at all levels, may be either helpful or harmful to local development efforts, and that tailored strategies grounded in public-private cooperation can be effective.

No one yet knows what sorts of brownfields strategies will most effectively advance minority community or any other interests in the long run. Experiences at individual sites may be so diverse, their evolution so continuous, and the number of arguably relevant variables so large that future efforts at comprehensive, persuasive, and prescriptive evaluation will founder. For the time being, we are clearly far from a time when anything like definitive assessment is possible. Thus far federal policymakers have understandably concentrated on the immediate challenges of getting the program up and running, and on reassuring communities (including communities of color) that their involvement is genuinely desired and essential to the program's success.

Training Initiatives

If federal agencies (largely through federal dollars) can mainly serve as hopeful catalysts for brownfields redevelopment and related job creation, they can perhaps play a similar role in preparing community residents for whatever jobs happen to be available in a given labor market. Both the government and communities envision residents learning marketable environment-related skills, and perhaps even participating in nearby site remediation, as a possible pathway to more and better long-term employment. The EPA and the National Institute for Environmental Health Sciences (NIEHS) are active on the job-training front, both separately and in tandem.

The EPA is attempting to serve the environmental justice vision of opportunity largely in the context of a broader overture to the nation's community colleges. Under a cooperative agreement with the EPA, the Hazardous Materials Training and Research Institute (HMTRI), an organization established in 1987 by two eastern Iowa community colleges, works to stimulate the participation of two-year colleges in brownfields redevelopment.[20] When the EPA announces a brownfields pilot grant, HMTRI contacts the relevant EPA regional office to determine whether community colleges in the pilot area want assistance in recasting themselves to take advantage of the opportunity. As HMTRI announced on its World Wide Web page: "It is expected that there will be many environmental jobs in the brownfields areas. There will be a need for environmental technicians to sample the areas believed to be contaminated, for lab technicians to test the samples, for technicians to clean up the contaminated areas, and for compliance officers to ensure the areas do not become re-contaminated when the area is reused."[21]

Since 1995 HMTRI has held several workshops around the country where community college representatives learned what brownfields are and how their respective institutions might plug into useful information networks and shape responsive programs. HMTRI tries to assure that community colleges serving largely minority clientele are included in the sessions and that they have ample access to HMTRI's contacts and expertise. Its fourth such workshop, in December 1996, was held in Boston, with Roxbury Community College, a historically black school, serving as the host institution.

HMTRI's mission is both to facilitate effective training and to help bolster community colleges as institutions. A guiding assumption is that brownfields redevelopment can effectively harmonize multiple goals. As Steve Fenton and Mike Senew of HMTRI write:

> If the Brownfields Initiative proceeds as anticipated, three positive outcomes will occur. First, the contaminated Brownfields sites will be cleaned up, reducing hazards to the citizens who live in these communities. Second, local citizens will be trained for new environmental and nonenvironmental jobs. And third, formerly abandoned properties will be redeveloped and returned to the tax rolls. Community colleges stand to gain not only an economic benefit from providing the training but also recognition for playing a major role in a project that brings significant benefits to the community.[22]

The NIEHS effort, known as the Minority Worker Training Program, began in the wake of the executive order and builds on a larger and somewhat older effort established under the 1986 Superfund Amendments and Reauthorization Act (SARA).[23] SARA authorized funds for the education and training of workers engaged in activities related to hazardous waste management. In the first seven years of that larger program, awardees reported training more than 350,000 participants.[24]

Through the intervention of then-chairman Louis Stokes (D-Ohio), the House Appropriations subcommittee with jurisdiction over the EPA budget added $3 million to the $20 million in so-called pass-through funding for NIEHS's Superfund worker training. As the committee report explained, the program would ideally serve both environmental and equal opportunity goals:

> The Committee recognizes that, as the demand for cleaning up the environment continues . . . there is a parallel demand for workers to perform the multiple tasks necessary to achieve environmental improvements. Assuring an adequate workforce to perform these tasks will require an aggressive and coordinated program of

recruitment, training, and service delivery. The nature of these jobs . . . is such that they require substantial level of training.

The Committee realizes that while efforts are underway to address these needs, there is growing consensus that these efforts are not adequate to meet current and projected needs for environmental workers. The scope of this need includes technicians, as well as doctoral-level physical and biological scientists. At the same time the Committee is aware that there is a large population of males, ages 18–25, in urban communities impacted by environmental pollutants who are unemployed because they lack the skills and knowledge required for many of the available career opportunities.

The Committee urges the agency to establish a series of national pilot programs to test a range of strategies for the recruitment and training of young persons, who live near hazardous waste sites or in the community at risk of exposure to contaminated properties, for work in the environmental field. . . .[25]

Mindful of the complex array of deficiencies facing the targeted constituency, the committee noted the variety of technical and basic skills it hoped the program would instill where appropriate—preemployment job training; literacy; life skills; construction skills; training in the abatement of hazardous waste, lead, and asbestos; and so on. This should be done, moreover, while allowing for "partnerships or subagreements with academic and other institutions, with a particular focus on historically black colleges and universities, and public schools located in or nearby the impacted area to provide pre-math, science or other related education to program participants prior to or concurrent with entry into the training program."[26]

With such expansive multiobjective language, anchored in a natural desire to squeeze the maximum impact out of a few million dollars in additional funding, the House committee created an obvious source of complications for future program administration. For not one but three trouble sites—disadvantaged young workers, community environmental problems, community educational institutions—were to remain targets of program implementation.

In November 1995 NIEHS announced the first seven recipients of its new minority worker training program cooperative agreements.[27] Its operating locations were widely dispersed and, as mandated by Congress, heavy on participation by minority institutions. These included: Jackson State University in Mississippi (in collaboration with the University of Alabama at Birmingham and a labor union); a joint San Francisco–Cleveland effort, again with significant labor participation; a New York–New Jersey award; a consortium led by the Carpenters Health and Safety Fund aimed at minority youth in four cities (New Orleans, Las Vegas, Los Angeles, and Minneapolis); a program based in southeast Chicago; and one for both Baltimore and Washington, D.C. Two well-known environmental justice scholar-activists and collaborators, Robert Bullard of Clark Atlanta University and Beverly Hendrix Wright of Xavier University in Louisiana, won funding to work with youth from "environmentally impacted neighborhoods" in Atlanta and New Orleans. As one might expect in light of Bullard's and Wright's prior criticisms of traditional environmentalism, their proposal laid a conspicuously strong emphasis on community involvement.[28]

Assuming that funds were forthcoming, the EPA planned to fill some of the gap left by the NIEHS training effort with a Superfund Jobs Training Initiative (SuperJTI).[29] The program consists of two "tiers," the first a basic training program, the second a more advanced effort linked to the Department of Labor's registered apprenticeship program. The EPA wants to encourage contractors to hire candidates who have completed the first tier's entry-level program. The second tier would provide more in-depth training, including the completion of "at least 2,000 hours of on-the-job training in a variety of skills in one particular occupation."[30] The EPA wants to model tier two after HUD's Step-Up Program, which includes apprenticeship training for housing residents. While SuperJTI is not officially labeled as a "minority" initiative, the EPA is clearly anxious to promote awareness of the program within communities of color.

As with the brownfields redevelopment initiative it is clearly too early to evaluate the EPA and NIEHS training initiatives. But it was apparent long before their creation that the sponsoring agencies, the funded institutions, and the target populations would all face daunting, and possibly insuperable, hurdles. At the most abstract level, means and ends were certain to be hard, if not impossible, to disentangle. It is clear from the congressional subcommittee report that an implicit purpose of the programs is to help sustain and strengthen provider institutions, a focus that can, as a practical matter, easily compete with distant and hard-to-measure employment goals as a focus.

It remained unclear what precisely would constitute failure or success on the part of recipient institutions. What level of retention in the programs would be judged too low? What length of employment or level of compensation would count as a good or bad placement? Does the environmental justice perspective's determination to assure that minority youth will not become fodder for high risk "dirty" jobs mean that even an economically remunerative placement might be deemed a failure for having resulted in some greater hazard exposure than would otherwise have occurred? Will future program evaluation accommodate the concept of a "risk premium"—allowing some workers to receive compensation for bearing risks that others do not?[31] In view of its determined avoidance of tradeoff questions, the environmental justice movement is unlikely to shed much light on such matters.

Participants in an NIEHS-sponsored technical workshop held at Cuyahoga Community College in January 1995 learned of many implementation pitfalls. Not surprisingly the federal Department of Energy (DOE) found it easiest to increase minority hiring at its facilities to levels approaching the minority population of the surrounding counties mainly in locales where the minority population was relatively low. In cities, however, DOE made less headway.[32] The Cleveland Lead Hazard Abatement Center explained that employment in hazard control tended to be concentrated in public and HUD-subsidized private housing, with "very little work [available] in the unsubsidized, private market."[33] Lead abatement would, it was said, not have much potential as a free-standing specialty, but would have to be "integrated into both the housing renovation and environmental remediation fields where trainees can learn broader and more marketable skills."[34] The leaders of the Environmental Sites Training Support Project at the Alice Hamilton Occupational Center in Washington, D.C. (which would later in the year receive one of the seven cooperative agreement awards) noted that the center had failed initially to make clear to early recruits that they would not learn enough to open their own environmental remediation firms, an omission that contributed to attrition among early classes.[35] The Alice Hamilton staff reported that sixty people had enrolled in their program, with fifty-two completing it. On the other hand "the intermittent nature of the employment remained a problem" and "it had to be impressed upon graduates that they would need to be persistent about calling in for work. Another problem was that the local housing authority had made a commitment to obtain jobs for the graduates and had not done so."[36] Motivation among the sometimes homeless trainees was said to be "inspirational" despite the often unsupportive and violence-ridden environments in which they had to function.

The Trouble with Training

Although it is possible to find employment training programs with good reputations—an oft-cited example is the mostly Mexican-American Center for Employment Training (CET) in San Jose, California—their overall track record inspires caution, to say the least, regarding prospects for effective *environment-related* job training.[37] Although careful to stress methodological difficulties impeding definitive evaluation, knowledgeable academic observers overwhelmingly view the overall impact of such programs as modestly positive, at best. Roberta M. Blank of Northwestern University writes that "there is still a great deal we don't know about how to run effective job training programs for disadvantaged workers, particularly for men and youth. Current research indicates that the benefits of job training efforts for these populations are at best uncertain."[38] Blank is candid about the political effects of this shaky record:

Particularly in a period when less skilled adult male workers are experiencing significant wage declines and related declines in labor market participation, the lack of a job training program for disadvantaged male workers that makes a large difference in their labor market participation or earnings levels is discouraging. Certainly the lack of documented success in this area is one reason that policymakers have been reluctant to fund major expansions of job training programs aimed broadly at the disadvantaged population.[39]

Robert I. Lerman offers a similarly depressing assessment of training programs targeted at disadvantaged youth. "Recent and careful studies of diverse targeted youth training programs," writes Lerman, "indicate that the programs achieved little to raise the long-term job success of disadvantaged youth participants."[40] W. Norton Grubb likewise discouragingly summarizes the job training experience to date:

> The cost-benefit analyses that have been done show that the social benefits usually (but not always) outweigh the costs, so that most of these programs are worth doing in a cost-benefit sense. One might conclude that job training has been successful and should be continued. However, the gains in employment and earnings are quite small from a practical standpoint: they are insufficient to move individuals out of poverty or off welfare; their effects very often decay over time, so that even the small benefits are short-lived; and, as they are currently constructed, they certainly do not give individuals a chance at middle-class occupations or incomes. In my interpretation, therefore, the successes of job training programs have been quite modest, even trivial. . . .[41]

Both Lerman and Grubb view most past job training efforts as too modest, too brief, and too disconnected from other employment support structures to do much good. Yet both remain persuaded that the social goals driving such program are far too important to abandon. Both want to strengthen linkages between schooling, training, and careers. Lerman advocates an integrated youth apprenticeship system (particularly for noncollege youth); Grubb supports a unified "ladder" of education, training, and employment experiences. Both see the School-to-Work Opportunities Act, signed into law in May of 1994, as a likely vehicle for the kind of transformations they advocate.

Given creativity and adequate resources, the environmental milieu might conceivably help the United States improve upon its often dismal record in employment training. If it does so, it might promote one of the main goals of environmental justice advocacy.

Uncertain Opportunity

Overall prospects facing environment-related (and thus environmental justice-responsive) policies to enhance economic opportunity are unclear. Brownfields revitalization is politically compelling and seems to have gotten off to a sound enough start. But as a policy driven by private sector incentives and intended mostly to heal widely scattered wounds, it seems unlikely to make much of a dent on poverty or the catastrophic problem of concentrated joblessness.

Some of the most careful and insightful students of urban social problems put little emphasis on economic development as a way to assist what William Julius Wilson has called "the truly disadvantaged," those persons comprising what is often called "the urban underclass."[42] Wilson sees job readiness and job search assistance as components of an overall national attack on joblessness in the urban ghetto.[43] But almost in the same breath Wilson also observes that "the central problem facing inner-city workers is not improving the flow of information about the availability of jobs, or getting to where the jobs are, or becoming job-ready. The central problem is that the demand for labor has shifted away from low-skilled workers because of structural changes in the economy."[44]

Imparting skills to those workers or potential workers most conspicuously lacking them would be a partial answer, if only we knew how to do so reliably. We do not. A major new public sector jobs program may be a partial answer, but a coalition of union and conservative opposition would probably preclude it, even if the jobs paid low wages. Higher wage jobs would likely end up being taken by middle-class, or experienced but displaced workers (some of them, to be sure, members of racial minority groups).[45]

Neither environmental justice activists nor environmental programs can do much about any of this. They have instead concentrated on making sure that community concerns and voices are not left out of the political discourse over brownfields revitalization. That, at least, is within their power.

Most significantly, environmental justice activism generally fails to confront the inevitable tradeoffs between economic opportunity and environmental risks. These risks are, in the grand scheme of things, mostly relatively low and manageable. Easy slogans do not adequately speak to the fates of communities that certainly want to avoid undue risk but that also need industrial development to provide jobs and local opportunity. What does environmental justice say, for example, to the residents of the predominantly black Louisiana town of Convent? In 1997–98 many of them anxiously awaited construction of a proposed plastics plant, only to see the EPA delay approval as a result of lobbying by an activist coalition that was probably unrepresentative of community sentiment.[46] If environmental justice means simply taking a harder look than otherwise might have been taken at the full array of costs and benefits of an action, that is probably to the good. But if it means blocking any facility that any person or group opposes with a cry of "environmental racism," then environmental policy will have taken a path that is all but certain to produce its own victimization of minorities.

Industrial siting is not the only place where a careful consideration of costs and benefits is warranted. Just as surely the democratized policymaking that grassroots environmental activists generally seek has both benefits and costs. These will be discussed in the final chapter.

6

PROSPECTS

BOTH ENVIRONMENTAL justice advocacy and the institutional change that has been, or might be, spawned by it are integral to a broader debate on environmental policy reform. This larger contest pits alternative *rationalizing* and *democratizing* reform perspectives against one another, prompting politicians and government officials to search for ways to straddle, if not completely reconcile, the two points of view. Environmental justice advocacy is a version of the democratizing critique that gives voice to a range of minority and low-income community concerns, some of which are not fundamentally environmental in the narrow sense. Problems identified by the rationalizing critique are de-emphasized, ignored, and possibly even exacerbated by democratizing changes. On the other hand, rationalizing approaches tend to downplay or overlook the social aspirations and popular emotions that underlie a democratizing focus. The conflict between these two reform perspectives is among the most serious challenges facing environmental policy.

Environmental policy has received considerable rationalizing criticism over the past two decades, with economists and economic modes of thought predominating. The economist's version has been that regulation is often wasteful because program ends and means display insufficient regard for, or analysis of, the social costs imposed by regulation. From this perspective such tools as cost-benefit and cost-effectiveness analysis, as well as market-like approaches to regulation have been too seldom used or accorded insufficient weight.[1]

A different kind of rationalizing critique, though respectful of the need to address costs and benefits formally when possible, encompasses a broader set of concerns: the discordant, meandering, and occasionally even panic-stricken character of regulatory politics and policy. From this point of view, the waste afflicting environmental regulation springs from a general failure to: (a) set priorities grounded in the severity or pervasiveness of problems, (b) define and adhere to consistent approaches among issues and agencies, and (c) remediate risk only to an extent deemed reasonable in light of the relevant costs and benefits.

This broader notion of rationalizing reform is addressed by Supreme Court Associate Justice Stephen Breyer. In his book *Breaking the Vicious Circle: Toward Effective Risk Regulation*, Breyer identifies three central problems plaguing risk regulation.[2] One he describes as tunnel vision, or "the problem of the last 10 percent." As Breyer elaborates:

> The regulating agency considers a substance that poses serious risks, at least through long exposure at high doses. It then promulgates standards so stringent—insisting, for example, upon rigidly strict site cleanup requirements—that the regulatory action ultimately imposes high costs without achieving significant additional safety benefits. A former EPA administrator put the problem succinctly when he noted that about 95 percent of the toxic material could be removed from waste sites in a few months, but years are spent trying to remove the last little bit.[3]

This is especially wasteful insofar as the risks associated with "the last 10 percent" are often held to be remarkably, even vanishingly, low. For example, Breyer asks: "Should the EPA have set a standard for transformers leaking PCB-laden mineral oil so low as to require the expenditure of $140 million to avoid health risks considerably lower than those accompanying eating a raw mushroom?"[4] But as noted in chapter 4, it is precisely such remote but involuntarily borne risks that the public is likely to dread most and demand to see eliminated.

Breyer's second and third problems are random agenda selection and inconsistency. By random agenda selection Breyer means the tendency for regulatory and political attention to be directed at general problems and specific substances with little coherent rationale. Instead an array of competing forces (for example, media coverage, lawsuits, congressional machinations, funding constraints, ongoing inter-agency debates) drive the creation of agendas and the setting of priorities. It is extraordinarily difficult to pursue a strategy of "worst things first" in such a setting. By inconsistency, Breyer means the different evaluative approaches embraced by agencies and a lack of coordination among them. Agencies have tended to proceed alone, chemical by chemical.

Breyer's proposed solution to these various problems is an enhancement of coordinating expertise. He suggests establishing "a new career path that would provide a group of civil servants with experience in health and environmental agencies, Congress, and OMB" as well as a "small, centralized administrative group, charged with a rationalizing mission, whose members would embark upon this career path."[5] Breyer is drawn to this alternative as more practical than deregulation or changes in Congress or the courts. Although the competence he proposes to nurture is not narrowly economic, Breyer is comfortable with the notion that the most rigorous possible analyses of risks, costs, benefits, and alternatives are a central resource on which regulatory policymakers must draw.

Breyer is hardly alone in his taste for a rationalizing reform that goes beyond economic analysis. In addition, widespread appreciation of the scientific uncertainty pervading environmental regulation has brought calls for access by policymakers, and by the Environmental Protection Agency in particular, to better scientific analysis. Advocates for a proposed National Institute for the

Environment, intended "to improve the scientific basis for making decisions on environmental issues," are animated by a similar rationalizing spirit.[6] Faith in expertise (whether scientific or economic) is by no means universal. For one thing, the data and interpretive tools necessary to address many problems are typically very limited. Another reason is that science and other forms of "rational analysis" cannot resolve what are ultimately value questions; they may even be a way of injecting values into decisionmaking without appearing to do so. This is particularly likely to the extent that the costs of an action are easily quantified while benefits are not, or when the easiest data to obtain and interpret favor one course of action whereas more elusive information (such as data on long-term health effects) might push decisionmaking in a different direction. Calls for more and better scientific studies may, if successful, simply generate more information than policymaking institutions can reasonably digest given their available resources. For example, John Wargo, a strong critic of the traditional regime of pesticide regulation, observes that "by the mid-1990s, EPA was overwhelmed with responses to its comprehensive request during the 1980s for more current environmental fate and toxicity data."[7]

Ironically one place where science and technology frequently engender strong skepticism is within the contemporary university, among scholars (rarely scientists themselves) who embrace postmodern ideas and attitudes. A radical strain of environmental philosophy also holds science largely responsible for the alienation of humankind from nature.[8] While the direct influence of such ideas and attitudes on environmental decisionmaking is no doubt limited, they nevertheless augment a general suspicion of elites, an unease with industrial capitalism (especially as pursued by large corporations), and a conviction that citizen perspectives are inadequately represented in decisionmaking.

These stances constitute the core of the malleable and improvisational overall critique that Andrew Szasz labels "radical environmental populism" or "ecopopulism."[9] The unwieldy list of seventeen principles cobbled together in October 1991 remain as close as the environmental justice segment of ecopopulism has come to a foundational or motivating text. Environmental justice proponent Bunyan Bryant acknowledges that "the literature is conspicuously without definitions" of environmental racism, equity, and justice, a state of affairs that encourages grassroots activists and their allies to employ the various terms more or less as they see fit.[10] Szasz observes that ecopopulism generally "has not settled on a single, clear political ideology" but rather displays "an untroubled eclecticism, a coexistence of multiple political symbol systems that have little in common except that they can be mobilized to legitimate a position of radical critique and activism."[11] However, adds Szasz, "the clearest and most consistent ideology of the movement is a . . . populism that depicts American history as, most centrally, a struggle of the small people against big government and big business."[12]

The central political project of ecopopulism is to amplify and empower the collective voices of ordinary citizens. This stance opposes not only corporate power but also its perceived handmaidens in science and technology. From this perspective science and scientific findings may be helpful but may also provide a distraction or, even worse, ammunition for the enemy. That is why grassroots environmental activists regularly counsel communities to be wary of science in general, and institution-based epidemiologic analysis in particular. Instead, it is argued, communities should stress political mobilization, augmented by "popular epidemiology." For example, a volume sponsored by the Citizens Clearinghouse for Hazardous Waste (run by former Love Canal activist Lois Gibbs) advises:

> Relying on the strength of scientific information rather than organizing can . . . cause problems. For one thing, it leads to "dueling experts syndrome" instead of campaigns based on common sense. Dueling experts syndrome can start when a local group brings in one scientist who says the community has a dioxin problem. Then the government or dioxin-polluting corporation brings in two other experts who say there is no problem and no cause for alarm. Members of the community then become confused because they are not sure who is right, and because most people don't understand the technical arguments or the jargon used.

When the dueling experts syndrome occurs at public meetings, the community loses interest. Members have no role to play, they can't engage in the discussions, and they have no say since the fight is now in the boxing ring of science.[13]

In a 1996 issue of the *Indigenous Environmental Network News*, which concentrates on matters of concern to Native American communities, Linda King of the Environmental Health Network offers similar advice:

There have been many communities who have had "cancer clusters" who are, after many years, still trying to prove that their environmental problems are the cause for these "cancer clusters." If your community is poor, lower middle class, in the south, rural, or minority you can pretty much expect to have your "cancer cluster" explained away by lifestyle, poor eating habits, alcohol consumption, or smoking. You can also expect the health departments to explain away your research results, telling you that the population surveyed was too small or too large, or that the right kinds of questions were not asked. Many communities have gotten their wish and their state or local health departments have become involved. This has backfired in every case that I am aware of. There are long delays in getting started. Information is made unavailable to the local group because of confidentiality. The local group no longer has a choice as to who is interviewed, which subdivision is used and how the results are arrived at. When it is no longer in your control you can be assured you are not going to be happy with the results and not aware of how those results were arrived at.[14]

As these comments suggest, the democratizing orientation in environmental policy reform assesses progress not by the conventional expertise brought to bear, nor by the extent to which decisions are harmonized, nor by the promotion of efficiency (in any sense). Rather, ecopopulists gauge success largely by standards of inclusiveness, community comfort and legitimacy, and fidelity to democratic practice.

By contrast, traditional public lobby activism remains more hospitable to formal analysis, which it is often well prepared to exploit. The Health Research Group, a Ralph Nader–affiliated advocacy organization headed for many years by an indefatigable physician, Sidney Wolfe, avidly embraces science and technical analysis as vital for helping to rein in corporate behavior. The organization has regularly employed scientific findings to promote stringent enforcement by the Food and Drug Administration and other regulatory bodies.[15]

As noted earlier, this Washington-based and staff-driven brand of activism differs significantly from grassroots groups arising out of particular communities and site-level disputes. The latter tend to have a narrower focus, an even greater mistrust of the establishment, and frequently a more militant style. At the true grassroots level, "useful" expertise is comprehensible among friends and neighbors, directly addresses their concerns, and helps them attain leverage over local debates and decisions. A common strategic yearning among grassroots activists (and among academics committed to social justice) is to identify and attract sympathetic scientists and technicians who can help empower the community.[16] While public lobby adherents such as Nader and Wolfe bridle at possible conflicts of interest among scientific and technical personnel (conflicts emanating especially from private sector attachments), grassroots activists, more despairing that anything resembling real objectivity is achievable, often aim merely to recruit their "own pool of scientific experts." As Cindy F. Kleiman of the American Council on Science and Health astutely observes, this is virtually "a recommendation *for* conflict of interest" albeit of a politically useful sort.[17]

Conceptual Drawbacks of Environmental Justice

From a rationalizing perspective, a major problem with the environmental justice version of the democratizing critique is that, like ecopopulism more generally, it threatens to worsen the problem of environmental policy's missing priorities. As Walter Rosenbaum elaborates:

> Like the man who mounted his horse and galloped off in all directions, the EPA has no constant course. With responsibility for administering nine separate statutes and parts of four others, the EPA has no clearly mandated priorities, no way of allocating scarce resources among different statutes or among programs within a single law. Nor does the EPA have a congressional charter, common to most federal departments and agencies, defining its broad organizational mission and priorities. . . .
>
> Congress has shown little inclination to provide the EPA with a charter or mandated priorities, in good part because the debate sure to arise on the relative merit and urgency of different environmental problems is an invitation to a political bloodletting most legislators would gladly avoid. Intense controversy would be likely among states, partisans of different ecological issues, and regulated interests over which problems to emphasize; the resulting political brawl would upset existing policy coalitions that themselves were fashioned with great difficulty. Moreover, setting priorities invites a prolonged, bitter debate over an intensely emotional issue: should the primary objective of environmental protection be to reduce public risks associated with environmental degradation as much as seems practical or—as many environmentalists fervently believe—is the goal to eliminate all significant forms of pollution altogether?[18]

Environmental justice inevitably enlarges this challenge of missing priorities, and for similar reasons. As noted earlier, the movement is a delicate coalition of local and ethnic concerns unable to narrow its grievances for fear of a similar "political bloodletting."[19] Overt de-emphasis or removal of any issue or claim would prompt the affected coalition members (for example, groups, communities, or tribes) to disrupt or depart it. And chances are they would not leave quietly but with evident resentment and perhaps accusatory rhetoric directed at the persons and organizations remaining. Real priority-setting runs contrary to radical egalitarian value premises, and no one (perhaps least of all a strong democratizer) wants to be deemed a victimizer.

Therefore movement rhetoric argues that *no* community should be harmed and that *all* community concerns and grievances deserve redress. Scholar-activist Robert Bullard proposes that "the solution to unequal protection lies in the realm of environmental justice for all Americans. No community, rich or poor, black or white, should be allowed to become a 'sacrifice zone.'"[20] When pressed about the need for environmental risk priorities, and about how to incorporate environmental justice into priority setting, Bullard's answer is a vague plea for nondiscrimination, along with a barely more specific call for a "federal 'fair environmental protection act'" that would transform "protection from a privilege to a right."[21]

Bullard's position is fanciful and self-contradictory, but extremely telling. He argues essentially that the way to establish environmental priorities is precisely by guaranteeing that such priorities are impossible to implement. This is symptomatic of a movement for which untrammeled citizen voice and overall social equity are cardinal values. Bullard's position also epitomizes the desire of movement intellectuals to avoid speaking difficult truths (at least in public) to their allies and constituents.

Ironically, in matters of health and risk, environmental justice poses a potentially serious, if generally unrecognized, danger to the minority and low-income communities it aspires to help. By discouraging citizens from thinking in terms of health and risk priorities (that is, by taking the position, in effect, that every chemical or site against which community outrage can be generated is equally hazardous), environmental justice can deflect attention from serious hazards to less serious or perhaps trivial ones.

Activists highlight the hypothetical hormone-disrupting effects of ambient dioxin levels, the possibility that any landfill can someday leak, and that incinerators might cause cancer. But this mobilize-against-intrusive-demon-technologies model of activism can target something like tobacco (or other largely behavioral hazards) only on the rare occasions when a visible external villain is conveniently present. R. J. Reynolds was in January 1990 when it prepared to test-market a new menthol cigarette, to be called Uptown, in Philadelphia's black neighborhoods. Reynolds made no effort to hide its intent to pitch the new brand explicitly to black smokers. The local American Cancer Society and many other groups coalesced in opposition. They soon received decisive help from a potent ally. The top federal health official, Secretary of Health and Human Services Louis Sullivan, an African-American hematologist, publicly derided Reynolds for promoting a "culture of cancer" among minorities during a speech at a University of Pennsylvania building dedication. Proclaimed Sullivan: "We must resist the unworthy efforts of the tobacco merchants to earn profits at the expense of the health and well-being of our poor and minority citizens." Although Sullivan had expected to mount an extended campaign against Reynolds, the company announced less than twenty-four hours after the speech that plans for Uptown had been canceled.[22]

Occasions for this sort of dramatic mobilizing are, by themselves, too rare to serve as a viable basis for healthier communities. Even though collective outrage can occasionally highlight a well-established cancer cause, such efforts must be superseded by more mundane, although often inadequate, efforts to induce healthy lifestyles. But the enormously important realm of behavioral risks generally finds scant role in an activism focused on prodding "the system" to yield concessions. Reliance on outrage is an exceedingly inefficient way to foster healthy minority and low-income communities.

From a health perspective the model's most serious drawback may be subtle opportunity costs. If one accepts that citizens inherently have limited time and energy to devote to their health, attention to distant or relatively minor health risks—however politically compelling—very likely means less attention for some more substantive health problems. And if one accepts that low-income citizens, in particular, have even fewer resources, and greater vulnerabilities, than more affluent citizens, then a focus on relatively low or unlikely risks could have a particularly insidious effect.

More frequent resort to a rationalizing, if not solely economic, perspective would encourage minority and low-income citizens and community leaders to think more carefully about priority-setting and myriad tradeoffs. Might widespread successes of NIMBY (not in my back yard) initiatives keep older and dirtier pollution sources active *longer* and thus adversely affect minority and low-income persons living adjacent to those sources? By the same token, does local insistence on full treatment at some Superfund sites (that is, the obsession with Breyer's "last ten percent") mean that risks elsewhere that might have been addressed under a more limited or flexible regime will not get attended to at all?

Such questions cannot be answered here, but the disinclination even to pose them is troubling. That a "nobody should suffer" position advocating maximum citizen engagement could have perverse effects will be painful for many even to consider. But honestly confronting the reality that no environmental amenity (with the possible exception of planetary gravity) is equally distributed may help make citizens more likely to ask hard questions about which inequities matter most. A more careful and comprehensive set of environmental equity comparisons than has been produced to date would probably conclude that there is reason for cheer on some fronts. After all, many Native Americans residing on tribal land, along with rural blacks, doubtless breathe far cleaner air than many far wealthier city dwellers. Of course, once broader social equity concerns—the real motivation for much environmental justice advocacy—are factored in, any clean air advantage may appear insignificant.

If Albert Nichols is right that failure to set environmental priorities based on risk has only worsened the inequities faced by minority and low-income communities, then there is even more compelling reason for greater reliance on a rationalizing approach. Writes Nichols in a direct critique of Bullard:

> If we accept the argument that the existing [politicized] approach has paid insufficient attention to the health and environmental risks

faced by minority communities, what does that then say about a risk-based alternative? *A strategy that emphasized attacking the largest and most easily reduced risks first would appear to represent a major gain for minority communities.* To the extent that such communities bear unusually high risks as a result of past discrimination or other factors, a risk-based approach would redirect more resources to these communities. Indeed, a risk-based approach would give highest priority to attacking precisely the kinds of problems that most concern Bullard.[23]

If conventional environmental justice advocacy cannot confront risk magnitudes honestly, it cannot help much in the assessment and management of tradeoffs, either of the risk/risk or risk/benefit varieties. The notion that attacking some risks may create others is largely foreign to environmental justice—beyond a fear that attacking the risk of poverty with industrial jobs may expose workers to hazardous conditions. A focus on community inclusion, although necessary to the ultimate acceptability of decisions, offers no automatic or painless way to sort through tradeoffs.[24]

When confronted with choices posing both risks and benefits—such as a proposed hazardous waste treatment facility that would create jobs, and impose relatively low risks, in a needy area—environmental justice offers, along with disgust that such horrendous choices exist, mainly community engagement and participation. But because such situations tend to stimulate multiple (and often harshly raised) local voices on *both* sides of the issue, activists are at pains to decide where (besides additional participation and deliberation) the community's interest lies. Because an activist group will be in close touch with both the fear of toxics and the hunger for economic opportunity, the organization itself may be torn. The locally one-sided issue presents far preferable terrain for activists. It should surprise no one that activists are anxious to deemphasize community-level disagreement of this sort. Nor is it surprising to learn from the head of a prominent environmental justice organization that her group tries to avoid situations that pose precisely these locally polarizing tradeoffs.[25] Faced with such tensions, environmental justice partisans may simply retreat into cant, attacking a system that facilitates "environmental blackmail," allowing disadvantaged communities to become "hooked on toxics."[26]

A further problem pervading environmental justice discourse is that some analysts insist on viewing the issue primarily through the prism of race, as environmental *racism*, and this is probably a misplaced focus. Although Clinton's executive order 12898 presents environmental justice in terms of both race and class, many movement partisans unhesitatingly assign race a dominant causal role leading to unfair outcomes.[27] Environmental historian Martin Melosi explains this insistence on a starkly racial analysis:

> The core view that race is at the heart of environmental injustice is borne of an intellectual and emotional attachment to the civil rights heritage of the past several decades. Few would deny—including the EPA—that poor people of color are *often* disproportionately impacted by *some* forms of pollution. But the qualifiers are significant. Outside the movement, there has been serious questioning: Is the issue really environmental racism or just poverty? Even within the movement there are those who cannot cleanly separate race and class in all cases.[28]

One additional, and especially disturbing, potential pitfall stems from an unwarranted focus on race as a dominant cause. Such analyses may encourage the dishearteningly alienated frame of mind that leads substantial numbers of African Americans to embrace racial conspiracy explanations. If people of color have been deliberately targeted for environmental poisons, then it stands to reason that they were "set up" for AIDS and crack cocaine and other evils as well.[29] Conversely, this conspiracy mindset doubtless contributes to the grassroots appeal of environmental racism rhetoric. America's legacy of slavery, segregation, and racism (epitomized in the health arena by the infamous Tuskegee syphilis study) has nurtured an understandable inclination among many African Americans to believe the worst of the system.[30]

Political and Policy Limitations of
Environmental Justice

Besides being characterized by significant drawbacks, environmental justice suffers from serious *limitations*. Although it has emerged as a significant theme in environmental policy discourse, environmental justice does not dominate or define environmentalism. The movement is too weak, has too few resources, and has too strong a local orientation to be a significant separate presence on such national and international matters as global warming, acid rain, airborne particulates, or the future of the electric car. On issues like these, environmental justice at best only adds to the general clamor for emission and waste reductions, and citizen involvement, on all fronts. An EPA administrator's commitment notwithstanding, the agency must attend to many other matters and to a wide array of constituency demands. Environmental justice cannot yet be described as a clear, durable, and primary goal for any national agency or significant interest group. It serves instead as an occasional, and maddeningly vague, political constraint, something to "take into account" (again, especially through mechanisms of community consultation) in the pursuit of other objectives.[31] Even where environmental justice has found a few footholds in the federal bureaucracy, it has stimulated mainly institutional promises of access and a fair hearing. Such promises are important but it will be hard to redeem them to the satisfaction of local activists.

Unlike the major traditional environmental organizations, the movement has little institutionalized presence in the nation's capital outside the federal agencies that have been ordered to pay attention to it by President Clinton. This is partly a matter of activist preference; many regard a major Washington identity as incompatible with the antibureaucratic and fundamentally populist thrust of the movement. A large Washington organization would tend to draw funds and attention away from the grassroots, where the real battles are waged. Such an entity would likely come into tension with communities and local activists insistent on speaking for themselves and unwilling to see "their" issues submerged within, or dropped from, a national organizational agenda.

It is thus understandable that when former EPA attorney Deeohn Ferris created the Washington Office on Environmental Justice, it remained tiny (Ferris and a couple of assistants) and focused on helping local communities formulate and implement effective strategies and find their bearings in Washington. In this respect Ferris's organization resembles the more elaborate Citizens Clearinghouse for Hazardous Waste (CCHW) in nearby Virginia, created by Lois Gibbs to provide "information, assistance, and solidarity" for grassroots groups.[32] Ecopopulism, whether black or white, generally does not really need regular Washington access to succeed at its crucial community-level advocacy function; local organizing has proved far more effective at blocking and curtailing targeted projects than recourse to Washington could ever be. As Gibbs and her CCHW assert: "the [federal] government won't stop the poisoning, but [local] organizing will."[33]

But on the federal stage environmental justice finds itself a warily regarded guest. As noted earlier, neither congressional Democrats nor a reasonably hospitable president (much less Republicans) have been anxious to disturb the existing environmental statutory regime on behalf of the movement. Even sympathetic institutional actors generally see assuring management sensitivity and a voice for communities, not grand statutory change, as the real challenge.

Environmental justice also has limited recourse to the judiciary or to conventional regulatory criteria. As previously noted, current equal protection doctrine elevates the bar for proving discrimination too high for almost any community. The EPA's Office of Civil Rights, which began reviewing dozens of local complaints for possible Title VI violations, had a hard time identifying them. Four years after the executive order, the office had yet to find an environmental justice complaint that appeared viable under the Civil Rights Act.

"Racism" makes a superb rallying cry, but it is unlikely to move a court unless considerable evidence is offered, more than is likely to be available in most instances, even if the Supreme Court opens the way for environmental justice lawsuits under Title VI of the Civil Rights Act. This is not just because racists have been careful to cover their tracks but because the actual historical dynamics of siting, and of the proximity of particular communities to particular sites, are genuinely complex and ambiguous. Communities of color may spring up over time near worrisome sites, lured by the prospect of jobs or cheap land. Even where past racist intent might have been a factor in siting, current policy offers limited tools for rectifying present-day effects. Regulators may often have scant justification for shutting down, or racheting down, discharges at a facility that complies with its current permits, whatever deficiencies might have characterized the siting process at some earlier time. Wholesale bans on new siting are not a plausible answer; at least from a rationalizing point of view, each new proposed facility must be evaluated on its merits. And, as noted in the preceding section, those merits inevitably turn into a discussion of tradeoffs. Does the facility provide jobs and needed treatment or disposal capacity? Can the community be effectively compensated for hosting it?[34] Can community concerns about possible negative impacts on health, property values, or overall quality of life be addressed early in the game through a relatively open dialogue that builds at least rudimentary trust?[35] As stressed already, environmental justice really specifies no answer to the question of what is best for a given community beyond the conviction that rigorous democratic practice and accountability are essential to a just outcome.

Although environmental justice has succeeded politically by repeated reference to several studies, empirical analysis has also proved difficult terrain. The evidence for racial inequity in site distribution is mixed, at best. And there is little reliable empirical evidence that people of color generally suffer adverse health effects related to industrial pollution at greater rates than whites. Moreover, *anyone* living in a big city is likely breathing dirtier air than anyone living elsewhere. Reasonable public concern, grounded in multiple scientific studies, exists about lead intake sufficient to impair intellectual function and development, especially among black and low-income children. It is also clear that, as with occupational chemicals generally, farmworker exposure is a serious matter. Such workers are likely to encounter pesticides and other agricultural chemicals at levels that are orders of magnitude above those affecting the public at-large. The difficulty of effectively according such issues the focus they deserve is one of the movement's most significant health-related weaknesses.

The social welfare aspirations that sustain much of the environmental justice agenda face perhaps the toughest sledding of all. Well-intended but limited and uncertain efforts are under way on a number of environment-related fronts (such as, job creation, job training, post-secondary education, and workforce diversity). Some identifiable individuals will doubtless benefit from each of these efforts, but there is no established fund of experience to suggest that environmental programs can be bent very much or very effectively to the service of targeted social welfare goals. Society does not know how to do a number of these things reliably, especially among the kinds of populations of greatest concern to environmental justice advocates. Moreover, it is all too obvious that the political will for major new redistributive efforts, even those carried out under an environmental rubric, is limited. The great untouchable "third rail" of American politics is not social security reform, as is so often claimed, but rather residential segregation, which doubtless under-lies at least some of what ends up being perceived or discussed as environmental injustice. In a useful development, some environmental justice activists have begun to talk about this. Unfortunately, they are also prone to a misleading conception of the status quo as kind of "apartheid," an emotionally charged term that may only help mask the complexity of residential patterns and the forces underlying them.[36]

The common vision of achieving integrated purposes simultane-ously—enabling community residents to remediate local environ-ments while gaining marketable skills for the longer term and paving the way for local jobs—is a fond one, but no one knows if it could be done with regular success. Very possibly it could not be, given the uncertainties, the uncontrollable variables, the multiplicity of actors, and the inadequate budgets that would be involved. The bipartisan appeal of "bricks and mortar" brownfields redevelopment may well have endowed it with political staying power. But the incentives and opportunities that initiate local redevelopment projects, and drive them to successful completion, will only rarely have much to do with helping environmental justice constituencies, especially the poor.

It is also unclear how, if at all, the economic opportunity theme meshes logically and practically with the NIMBY tendencies inherent in the democratizing focus. The former promotes clearing obstacles to investment, while the latter focuses on challenging unwanted new siting. Neither activists nor officials have explained clearly how policy should manage this tension. As the EPA and the Department of Justice contemplate greater reliance on Title VI and the National Environmental Policy Act as civic involvement tools, they would do well to consider the long-term implications for brownfields redevelopment as a opportunity-promoting initiative.

Achievements of Environmental Justice

Despite the serious problems discussed above, neither the record of environmental justice advocacy nor its prospects are uniformly bleak. For one thing, by helping to sustain grassroots environmentalism more generally, such advocacy may contribute valuable political support to the campaigns for both toxics use reduction and pollution prevention. While there are good reasons to challenge the federal Toxics Release Inventory (TRI) as an indicator of overall emissions, TRI has proven an undeniably effective tool for citizen-activists to encourage reduced emissions.[37] Environmental justice activists have long noted that pollution prevented need not be distributed to *any* community.[38] The EPA clearly embraces a linkage between prevention (which received a congressional stamp of approval in the 1990 Pollution Prevention Act) and pursuit of environmental justice.[39]

Advocates can also point to considerable concrete political success on at least two other fronts: coalition building and agenda-setting. As Martin Melosi acknowledges, the environmental justice movement "is playing a historic role in reintroducing 'equity' into the public and academic debate over environmental policy."[40]

The vast inclusiveness of environmental justice, both as vague concept and as heterogeneous movement, may play havoc with priority-setting but this remains an essential source of its political durability. Environmental justice facilitates coalition-building, since any conceivably environment-related claim, belief, decision, practice, or policy affecting any minority or low-income interest is fair game for inclusion. So long as mutual deference prevails regarding the objectives of various black, Latino, Asian-American, and Native American activists—objectives that include the avoidance of locally unwanted land uses, political recognition and participation, residential relocation, and much else besides—there exists the potential for a united front.

A further source of strength lies in a capacity for local mobilization inherent in perceived threats to health (and especially to the health of children) that citizens deem serious and believe to have been imposed on them. Environmental justice resolves the crucial political challenges of mobilization and coalition-building by emphasizing one general message: we are all under attack and must stand together to fight.

Environmental justice has succeeded not only at local mobilizing and coalition politics but also at the crucial task of political agenda-setting. The movement has won recognition from policymakers that concern for minority and low-income communities must be a consideration when certain kinds of decisions, such as siting choices in or near communities of color, are made. Policymakers in environment-related agencies throughout the federal government—from the Nuclear Regulatory Commission to the Forest Service—are demonstrating awareness of the executive order's mandate. There are at least anecdotal indications that some agency managers have begun raising questions about possible disparate impacts and the adequacy of community consultation during decisionmaking.

One cheering tale of bureaucratic thoughtfulness emerges from the Animal and Plant Health Inspection Service (APHIS), a part of the Department of Agriculture. In March 1995, after local consultation, APHIS decided that its boll weevil eradication program for the lower Rio Grande Valley should incorporate additional precautions to assure the most limited possible adverse impact on the very poor, Spanish-speaking residents. As the final environmental assessment notes:

> In the Lower Rio Grande Valley, a large number of colonias (subdivisions) exist adjacent to cotton fields. Concerns for these colonias relate to potential water contamination from factors including pesticide drift and pesticide runoff. Many of the colonias have limited or no access to clean running water. Although most colonias have access to public water supplies for drinking water, others (typically the newer ones) do not and residents may obtain their drinking water from irrigation ditches that drain surrounding agricultural fields. Houses in some colonias also may lack adequate shower/bath facilities. . . . Also, many of the colonias' houses lack air conditioning and good air ventilation.[41]

APHIS decided to employ malathion, the least toxic of the available pesticides, and employed quite conservative assumptions in assessing potential exposure. The program would also include careful monitoring of wind direction, allow spraying only outside generous buffer zones, employ global positioning system technology to gauge precisely where spraying had occurred, and pursue aggressive Spanish-language outreach to keep residents continually informed. In sum, APHIS was able to go "the extra mile" to further police a probably rather low risk to a population of special concern, and do so without controversy or unreasonable expense.

Environmental justice advocates are clearly winning concrete local victories. They have brought attention to places like Chester, Pennsylvania, and to the Kennedy Heights neighborhood of Houston, which in 1997 brought a widely publicized lawsuit against the Chevron Corporation for having allegedly wrought chronic illnesses among residents by leaving crude oil residues on property it once owned.[42] Pensacola's Escambia neighborhood won relocation away from "Mount Dioxin" just before the 1996 presidential election. In May 1997 the atomic safety and licensing board of the Nuclear Regulatory Commission (NRC) rebuffed an application to build a uranium enrichment plant between two African American neighborhoods in Louisiana. According to the board, the site selection process may have been unfair and did not adequately assess relevant environmental, social, and economic impacts.[43] In April 1998, just days after winning a partial reprieve from the NRC, Louisiana Energy Services announced the withdrawal of its license application "after more than seven years of effort and $34 million in costs."[44]

Although this essay concentrates on the *federal* response to environmental justice concerns, there has also been considerable activity in a number of state governments. But as would be expected, state experience varies considerably, especially regarding timing and the basic level of official attention exhibited. A 1995 letter of inquiry sent to the top environmental official of every state found some states (Maine, Idaho, and Montana) claiming little or no formal environmental justice activity, at least at that time.[45] At the other end of the spectrum resided states (Florida, Louisiana, Texas, and Oregon) with considerable activity—that is, they were at least aggressively discussing the issue—quite apart from more general and widespread advocacy of citizen participation and "fair share" initiatives. In May 1994 Florida enacted legislation creating an Environmental Equity and Justice Commission to make recommendations.[46] Texas set up an Environmental Equity and Justice Task Force in 1993.[47] Louisiana pursued environmental justice not only through its state advisory committee to the U.S. Commission on Civil Rights but also in 1993 legislation mandating the state Department of Environmental Quality to review the issue and report recommendations to the legislature.[48] In 1993 the director of the Oregon Department of Environmental Quality appointed an Environmental Equity Citizen Advisory Committee at the request of the governor. The resulting report, released in October 1994, stressed public participation and diversity.[49]

This much is clear: the environmental justice movement has significantly, if unevenly, transformed the political climate in which many kinds of actions will be considered, both in the federal government and in a growing number of states. If they ever were, racial minorities are no longer the "invisible man" of environmentalism.

Healthy and Livable Communities: Toward a New Dialogue

Grassroots environmentalism appears durable despite its deficiencies. Local concern for institutional accountability, equity, and responsiveness in the environmental realm are unlikely to diminish. Popular longing for greater democratic influence over large and distant institutions, and the sometimes hazardous technologies they employ or oversee, is quintessentially American. Moreover, grassroots environmental activists themselves are unlikely to alter what they do in any fundamental way. From their point of view, their primary failure has lain in not being effective enough at mobilizing citizens and helping them to challenge the system.

The larger context in which activists and citizens must function can and should change with the dissemination and institutionalization of alternative ideas. For most of the nearly two-decade history of the active environmental justice movement, discussion of priorities and tradeoffs has been largely set aside. Effort has focused instead on agenda-setting and coalition-building. Environmentalists and environmental policymakers have either paid scant attention to this failure or concentrated on making themselves (and whatever information they have to share) accessible, thereby demonstrating responsiveness and deflecting allegations of inattention and unfairness.

Emerging as they have mainly from the political left, academic students of environmental justice have tended to define their inquiry and commentary in line with their reflexive sympathy for democratic and redistributive aspirations, and their belief that uncertainty and ambiguity will always be manipulated by those in power. There has been understandable reluctance to criticize, even constructively, a movement that expresses the concerns of disadvantaged persons.

Ironically, part of the cure for what ails environmental justice today is a significantly enhanced discourse bringing new voices and concerns to the table. A rival conception of environmental justice, energized by an expanded audience asking new and in some cases uncomfortable questions is overdue. On the health front, traditional public health advocates, especially persons and groups with strong ties to minority and low-income communities, should began to make their voices, professions, and disciplines heard. With active engagement and leadership from health professionals, including the powerful bully pulpit of the surgeon general's office, a new "people of color community health movement" might bring renewed attention to the broad range of health problems disproportionately affecting minority communities (including industrial pollution, when warranted).[50]

Such an enterprise, driven by disease and death, instead of by fear of sites and chemicals, would for the most part challenge conventional environmental justice advocacy only indirectly, by raising more effectively the priority of matters like asthma management, farmworker chemical exposures, practical lead exposure control measures, and the further reduction of tobacco use (especially where that use is conspicuously greater than average). A guiding premise of such a health-based effort would be a conception of "the environment" as including any process, behavior, or substance one is likely to encounter. Attention by this new political vehicle and by policymakers to *indoor environments* (where people spend enormous amounts of time) and to *individual behavior* (which surely accounts for a large fraction of the overall risk the average person faces) would likely target health concerns among low-income and minority communities far more effectively than selective trolling for governmental and corporate environmental villains. While disproportionate impact would be a concern, the sheer size and pervasiveness of health effects within minority and low-income populations would weigh more heavily than "fairness"—especially if, by that word, one means simply highlighting every grievance and blocking any activity that stimulates one.

To facilitate priority setting, this alternative institution would have to be devised self-consciously, and with some "top-down" leadership, instead of embracing willy-nilly the scattered agendas of local groups. Such an entity would not exemplify perfect democracy and issue permeability in its own structure or agenda. But it would present offsetting advantages, promoting a more informed and reasoned democratic practice where it really counts: in local communities, which would thereby gain stronger guidance and assistance, especially for ever-critical educational and risk communication tasks.

One must bear in mind that both an advisory body, such as the National Environmental Justice Advisory Council (NEJAC), and a small office with no line authority, such as the Office of Environmental Justice (OEJ), are severely constrained by the larger institutional framework in which they are embedded. Neither can effectively address most health issues of importance in communities of color simply because most such matters lie beyond EPA's policy domain. Still, both NEJAC and the OEJ ought to pursue their respective missions with a greater sense of substantive environmental priorities, with more determination to attack "worst things first" than has generally been the case. It is important that they do so partly because they cannot productively attend to most of what is important on the health front, and partly because disadvantaged citizens need priorities even more than the better-off. Yet both NEJAC and the OEJ will almost certainly pursue the far less contentious path of a search for "procedural" priorities, emphasizing mechanisms by which *all* communities can more readily place their grievances on the table.

Meanwhile, a much broader notion than health—quality of life—wields a powerful claim as an environmental justice theme. But an obvious conceptual challenge posed by the quality of life rubric is definitional: criteria are hard to specify. Researchers at the University of Tennessee's Waste Management Research and Education Institute report that participants in state comparative risk projects are animated by an array of quality-of-life concerns, including "peace of mind, sense of community, and fairness to future generations."[51] Virtually any valued aspect of collective life may turn up in assessments of community concerns.[52]

The vagueness problem notwithstanding, such concrete complaints such as filth, noise, odors, congestion, and dilapidation are legitimately environmental, for they are public and collectively experienced burdens that offend the senses, depress the spirit, and exacerbate other problems.[53] Also clearly environmental are such challenges as a paucity of green space, recreational opportunities, and simple fresh air. Lack of access to such environmental amenities constitutes a compelling social equity problem for which effective citizen and community advocacy are not merely useful but essential.

These problems, and the skewed residential patterns that may underlie or intensify them, should be addressed directly rather than riding as hidden cargo aboard exaggerated or unsubstantiated assertions of risk and racism in siting and enforcement. It distorts the truth to describe as "racist" locational decisions by business firms that simply amount to rational business practices. Such practices include searching for cheap land, for infrastructure conveniences (that is, access to highways, rail lines, docks, pipelines, and other commercial amenities near which persons of modest means often reside), and for communities unlikely to oppose one's presence.[54]

In the final analysis, much of what animates environmental justice advocacy is an abiding hunger for livable communities. In this vein the "environmental racism" most worth confronting has historically restricted housing and occupational choices for many low-income and minority citizens, largely through government policies that have helped to place large distances between those choices and those citizens.[55] Indeed, not so long ago, Federal Housing Administration mortgage insurance policies regularly treated African Americans as a kind of human analogue to toxic waste.[56] Blacks were seen as a threat to a neighborhood's harmony, quality, and property values. As such they were to be avoided when possible.

Ironically, words like "preservation" and "stewardship," long associated with an elite brand of environmentalism, may be keys to a more thoughtful environmental justice discourse. As Richard Moe and Carter Wilkie recently observed, "some of the most encouraging

instances of neighborhood preservation today are occurring in historically African American neighborhoods, the kind of places written
off for decades by mortgage lenders and urban renewal policies."[57]

When are minority communities better off being assisted in such
redevelopment efforts? And when might their interests lie, instead,
in assisted evacuation to more affluent or nurturing premises?[58] Can
public policy rationally promote both approaches simultaneously
and without contributing to the suburban sprawl that so concerns
Moe and Wilkie? In a recent history of neighborhood antipoverty
initiatives Robert Halpern frames the issue well:

> The 1990s once again bring a federal government that is activist in
> spirit, if not in capacity. For the first time in over a decade the
> Department of Housing and Urban Development is struggling to
> figure out how to help inner-city neighborhoods and their residents.
> Should it focus on neighborhood revitalization per se; on providing
> inner-city residents the skills, transportation links, and job informa-
> tion that will improve their access to suburban jobs, but leave them
> the option of staying or leaving; on directly trying to "disperse"
> inner-city residents to other neighborhoods and communities; or
> perhaps on all three?[59]

These are foundational quality-of-life questions for environmental justice advocates and constituencies. But merely to recite them is
to realize that the EPA and state environmental authorities are woe-
fully inadequate places to look for anything like complete answers.

On the more narrowly technical matter of health (that is, the prevention of disease, disability, and premature death) environmental
and public health authorities at all levels must offer stronger guidance to local communities, addressing fear with facts and the best
possible analysis. Authorities must also engage communities and
activists alike in candid discussions of priorities and tradeoffs. What
kinds of environmental problems in minority and low-income communities are most deserving of the limited attention and funding
available? To what extent can such communities be effectively compensated for hosting risky facilities?[60]

Careful risk communication is never more important than when basic nutritional concerns raise frightening and confusing risk-benefit tradeoffs, especially among communities that may lack both the education and the media sophistication that facilitate thoughtful choice. If toxic residues contaminate fish, what reasonable guidance should one offer to minority communities that may consume larger than average quantities of fish?[61] (As toxicologists might put it, what dose makes the poison?) If some persons are to consume less of a given food, what risks and benefits characterize any likely nutritional substitutes? Otherwise we are at risk of addressing one problem by creating a worse one.

Deriving the appropriate information is only the beginning of communicating it effectively. A purely "top-down" model of communication is not workable. Local citizen cooperation is surely essential to effective risk communication and behavior change in disadvantaged communities.[62] The reason is simply that the necessary trust and behavioral reinforcement may prove elusive. Variations on a stereotypically middle-class (if largely apolitical) grass-roots institution, the support group, merit exploration in this regard. Efforts to help individuals likely will work better if the approach is not purely individualistic.[63]

Some difficult collective learning lies ahead. Local communities must appreciate that the environmental justice mantra of "multiple, cumulative, and synergistic risk" is sometimes more readily addressed with available knowledge once personal behavior and lifestyle choices are part of the picture. To cite one example, it is plausible that community effort might help address the risk of esophageal cancer associated with synergistic exposure to both alcohol and tobacco products.[64] People like Chicago activist and former NEJAC member Hazel Johnson must be educated away from the intuitively appealing, but hazardous, assumption that "light" smoking poses little health risk. African American women, in particular, must become far more aware of the "environment" that is propelling them into a quiet epidemic of obesity, with calamitous health consequences.[65]

Those who would advance social justice in the environmental realm, or through environmental policy tools, must begin thinking of better ways to discriminate—between the very important and the less important, between the deserving and the undeserving, between what is empirically defensible and what is not. The pursuit of justice requires the making of distinctions, not just the pursuit of rights and the flexing of advocacy muscle. Everyone must learn that while government has a vitally important role to play, we cannot simply legislate, regulate, litigate, or protest our way toward healthy and livable communities.

EXECUTIVE ORDER 12898

of Feb. 11, 1994 (59 F.R. 7629, Feb. 16, 1994)

Federal Actions to Address Environmental Justice in Minority Populations and Low-Income Populations

By the authority vested in me as President by the Constitution and the laws of the United States of America, it is hereby ordered as follows:

Section 1-1. Implementation.

1-101. Agency Responsibilities. To the greatest extent practicable and permitted by law, and consistent with the principles set forth in the report on the National Performance Review, each Federal agency shall make achieving environmental justice part of its mission by identifying and addressing, as appropriate, disproportionately high and adverse human health or environmental effects of its programs, policies, and activities on minority populations and low-income populations in the United States and its territories and possessions, the District of Columbia, the Commonwealth of Puerto Rico, and the Commonwealth of the Mariana Islands.

1-102. Creation of an Interagency Working Group on Environmental Justice. (a) Within 3 months of the date of this order, the Administrator of the Environmental Protection Agency ("Administrator") or the Administrator's designee shall convene an interagency Federal Working Group on Environmental Justice ("Working Group"). The Working Group shall comprise the heads of the following executive agencies and offices, or their designees: (a) Department of Defense; (b) Department of Health and Human Services, (c) Department of Housing and Urban Development; (d) Department of Labor; (e) Department of Agriculture; (f) Department of Transportation; (g) Department of Justice; (h) Department of the Interior; (i) Department of Commerce; (j) Department of Energy; (k) Environmental Protection Agency; (l) Office of Management and Budget; (m) Office of Science and Technology Policy; (n) Office of the Deputy Assistant to the President for Environmental Policy; (o) Office of the Assistant to the President for Domestic Policy; (p) National Economic Council; (q) Council of Economic Advisers; and such other Government officials as the President may designate. The Working Group shall report to the President through the Deputy Assistant to the President for Environmental Policy and the Assistant to the President for Domestic Policy.

(b) The Working Group shall: (1) provide guidance to Federal agencies on criteria for identifying disproportionately high and adverse human health or environmental effects on minority populations and low-income populations; (2) coordinate with, provide guidance to, and serve as a clearinghouse for, each Federal agency as it develops an environmental justice strategy as required by section 1103 of this order, in order to ensure that the administration, interpretation and enforcement of programs, activities and policies are undertaken in a consistent manner; (3) assist in coordinating research by, and stimulating cooperation among, the Environmental Protection Agency, the Department of Health and Human Services, the Department of Housing and Urban Development, and other agencies conducting research or other activities in accordance with section 33 of this order; (4) assist in coordinating data collection, required by this order; (5) examine existing data and studies on environmental justice; (6) hold public meetings as required in section 5502(d) of this order; and (7) develop interagency model projects on environmental justice that evidence cooperation among Federal agencies.

1-103. Development of Agency Strategies. (a) Except as provided in section 6-605 of this order, each Federal agency shall develop an agency wide environmental justice strategy, as set forth in subsections (b)–(e) of this section that identifies and addresses disproportionately high and adverse human health or environmental effects of its programs, policies, and activities on minority populations and low-income populations.The environmental justice strategy shall list programs, policies, planning and public participation processes, enforcement, and/or rulemakings related to human health or the environment that should be revised to, at a minimum: (1) promote enforcement of all health and environmental statutes in areas with minority populations and low-income populations; ensure greater public participation; (3) improve research and data collection relating to the health of and environment of minority populations and low-income populations; and (4) identify differential patterns of consumption of natural resources among minority populations and low-income populations. In addition, the environmental justice strategy shall include, where appropriate, a timetable for undertaking identified revisions and consideration of economic and social implications of the revisions.

(b) Within 4 months of the date of this order, each Federal agency shall identify an internal administrative process for developing its environmental justice strategy, and shall inform the Working Group of the process.

(c) Within 6 months of the date of this order, each Federal agency shall provide the Working Group with an outline of its proposed environmental justice strategy.

(d) Within 10 months of the date of this order, each Federal agency shall provide the Working Group with its proposed environmental justice strategy.

(e) By March 24, 1995 [as amended by Executive Order, January 30, 1995], each Federal agency shall finalize its environmental justice strategy and provide a copy and written description of its strategy to the Working Group. From the date of this order through March 24,

1995 [as amended by Executive Order, January 30, 1995], each Federal agency, as part of its environmental justice strategy, shall identify several specific projects that can be promptly undertaken to address particular concerns identified during the development of the proposed environmental justice strategy, and a schedule for implementing those projects.

(f) Within 24 months of the date of this order, each Federal agency shall report to the Working Group on its progress in implementing its agency wide environmental justice strategy.

(g) Federal agencies shall provide additional periodic reports to the Working Group as requested by the Working Group.

1-104. Reports to the President. Within 14 months of the date of this order, the Working Group shall submit to the President, through the Office of the Deputy Assistant to the President for Environmental Policy and the Office of the Assistant to the President for Domestic Policy, a report that describes the implementation of this order, and includes the final environmental justice strategies described in section 1103(e) of this order.

Sec. 2-2. Federal Agency Responsibilities for Federal Programs.

Each Federal agency shall conduct its programs, policies, and activities that substantially affect human health or the environment, in a manner that ensures that such programs, policies, and activities do not have the effect of excluding persons (including populations) from participation in, denying persons (including populations) the benefits of, or subjecting persons (including populations) to discrimination under, such programs, policies, and activities, because of their race, color, or national origin.

Sec. 3-3. Research, Data Collection, and Analysis.

3-301. Human Health and Environmental Research and Analysis. (a) Environmental human health research, whenever practicable and appropriate, shall include diverse segments of the population in epidemiological and clinical studies, including segments at high risk from environmental hazards, such as minority populations, low-income populations and workers who may be exposed to substantial environmental hazards.

(b) Environmental human health analyses, whenever practicable and appropriate, shall identify multiple and cumulative exposures.

(c) Federal agencies shall provide minority populations and low-income populations the opportunity to comment on the development and design of research strategies undertaken pursuant to this order.

3-302. Human Health and Environmental Data Collection and Analysis. To the extent permitted by existing law, including the Privacy Act, as amended (5 U.S.C. section 552a): (a) each Federal agency, whenever practicable and appropriate, shall collect, maintain, and analyze information assessing and comparing environmental and human health risks borne by populations identified by race, national origin, or income. To the extent practical and appropriate, Federal agencies shall use this information to determine whether their programs, policies, and activities have disproportionately high and adverse human health or environmental effects on minority populations and low-income populations;

(b) In connection with the development and implementation of agency strategies in section 1103 of this order, each Federal agency, whenever practicable and appropriate, shall collect, maintain and analyze information on the race, national origin, income level, and other readily accessible and appropriate information for areas surrounding facilities or sites expected to have a substantial environmental, human health, or economic effect on the surrounding populations, when such facilities or sites become the subject of a substantial Federal environmental administrative or judicial action. Such information shall be made available to the public, unless prohibited by law; and

(c) Each Federal agency, whenever practicable and appropriate, shall collect, maintain, and analyze information on the race, national origin, income level, and other readily accessible and appropriate information for areas surrounding Federal facilities that are: (1) subject to the reporting requirements under the Emergency Planning and Community Right to Know Act, 42 U.S.C. section 11001-11050 as mandated in Executive Order No. 12856; and (2) expected to have a substantial environmental, human health, or economic effect on surrounding populations. Such information shall be made available to the public, unless prohibited by law.

(d) In carrying out the responsibilities in this section, each Federal agency, whenever practicable and appropriate, shall share information and eliminate unnecessary duplication of efforts through the use of existing data systems and cooperative agreements among Federal agencies and with State, local, and tribal governments.

Sec. 4-4. Subsistence Consumption of Fish and Wildlife.

4-401. Consumption Patterns. In order to assist in identifying the need for ensuring protection of populations with differential patterns of subsistence consumption of fish and wildlife, Federal agencies, whenever practicable and appropriate, shall collect, maintain, and analyze information on the consumption patterns of populations who principally rely on fish and/or wildlife for subsistence. Federal agencies shall communicate to the public the risks of those consumption patterns.

4-402. Guidance. Federal agencies, whenever practicable and appropriate, shall work in a coordinated manner to publish guidance reflecting the latest scientific information available concerning methods for evaluating the human health risks associated with the consumption of pollutant bearing fish or wildlife. Agencies shall consider such guidance in developing their policies and rules.

Sec. 5-5. Public Participation and Access to Information.

(a) The public may submit recommendations to Federal agencies relating to the incorporation of environmental justice principles into Federal agency programs or policies. Each Federal agency shall convey such recommendations to the Working Group.

(b) Each Federal agency may, whenever practicable and appropriate, translate crucial public documents, notices, and hearings relating to human health or the environment for limited English speaking populations.

(c) Each Federal agency shall work to ensure that public documents, notices, and hearings relating to human health or the environment are concise, understandable, and readily accessible to the public.

(d) The Working Group shall hold public meetings, as appropriate, for the purpose of fact finding, receiving public comments, and conducting inquiries concerning environmental justice. The Working Group shall prepare for public review a summary of the comments and recommendations discussed at the public meetings.

Section 6-6. General Provisions.

6-601. Responsibility for Agency Implementation. The head of each Federal agency shall be responsible for ensuring compliance with this order. Each Federal agency shall conduct internal reviews and take such other steps as may be necessary to monitor compliance with this order.

6-602. Executive Order No. 12250. This Executive order is intended to supplement but not supersede Executive Order No. 12250, which requires consistent and effective implementation of various laws prohibiting discriminatory practices in programs receiving Federal financial assistance. Nothing herein shall limit the effect or mandate of Executive Order No. 12250.

6-603. Executive Order No. 12875. This Executive order is not intended to limit the effect or mandate of Executive Order No. 12875.

6-604. Scope. For purposes of this order, Federal agency means any agency on the Working Group, and such other agencies as may be designated by the President, that conducts any Federal program or activity that substantially affects human health or the environment. Independent agencies are requested to comply with the provisions of this order.

6-605. Petitions for Exemptions. The head of a Federal agency may petition the President for an exemption from the requirements of this order on the grounds that all or some of the petitioning agency's programs or activities should not be subject to the requirements of this order.

6-606. Native American Programs. Each Federal agency responsibility set forth under this order shall apply equally to Native American programs. In addition, the Department of the Interior, in coordination with the Working Group, and, after consultation with tribal leaders, shall coordinate steps to be taken pursuant to this order that address Federally recognized Indian Tribes.

6-607. Costs. Unless otherwise provided by law, Federal agencies shall assume the financial costs of complying with this order.

6-608. General. Federal agencies shall implement this order consistent with, and to the extent permitted by, existing law.

6-609. Judicial Review. This order is intended only to improve the internal management of the executive branch and is not intended to, nor does it create any right, benefit, or trust responsibility, substantive or procedural, enforceable at law or equity by a party against the United States, its agencies, its officers, or any person. This order shall not be construed to create any right to judicial review involving the compliance or noncompliance of the United States, its agencies, its officers, or any other person with this order.

William J. Clinton

THE WHITE HOUSE
February 11, 1994.

PRINCIPLES OF ENVIRONMENTAL JUSTICE

Adopted October 1991, Washington, D.C.

Preamble

We the people of color, gathered together at this multi-national People of Color Environmental Leadership Summit, to begin to build a national and international movement of all peoples of color to fight the destruction and taking of our lands and communities, do hereby re-establish our spiritual interdependence to the sacredness of our Mother Earth; to respect and celebrate each of our cultures, languages and beliefs about the natural world and our roles in healing ourselves; to insure environmental justice; to promote economic alternatives which would contribute to the development of environmentally safe livelihoods; and, to secure our political, economic and cultural liberation that has been denied for over 500 years of colonization and oppression, resulting in the poisoning of our communities and land and the genocide of our peoples, do affirm and adopt these Principles of Environmental Justice:

1. *Environmental justice* affirms the sacredness of Mother Earth, ecological unity and the interdependence of all species, and the right to be free from ecological destruction.

2. *Environmental justice* demands that public policy be based on mutual respect and justice for all peoples, free from any form of discrimination or bias.

3. *Environmental justice* mandates the right to ethical, balanced and responsible uses of land and renewable resources in the interest of a sustainable planet for humans and other living things.

4. *Environmental justice* calls for universal protection from nuclear testing, extraction, production and disposal of toxic/hazardous wastes and poisons and nuclear testing that threaten the fundamental right to clean air, land, water, and food.

5. *Environmental justice* affirms the fundamental right to political, economic, cultural and environmental self-determination of all peoples.

6. *Environmental justice* demands the cessation of the production of all toxins, hazardous wastes, and radioactive materials, and that all past and current producers be held strictly accountable to the people for detoxification and the containment at the point of production.

7. *Environmental justice* demands the right to participate as equal partners at every level of decision-making including needs assessment, planning, implementation, enforcement and evaluation.

8. *Environmental justice* affirms the right of all workers to a safe and healthy work environment, without being forced to choose between an unsafe livelihood and unemployment. It also affirms the right of those who work at home to be free from environmental hazards.

9. *Environmental justice* protects the right of victims of environmental injustice to receive full compensation and reparations for damages as well as quality health care.

10. *Environmental justice* considers governmental acts of environmental injustice a violation of international law, the Universal Declaration on Human Rights, and the United Nations Convention on Genocide.

11. *Environmental justice* must recognize a special legal and natural relationship of Native Peoples to the U.S. government through treaties, agreements, compacts, and covenants affirming sovereignty and self-determination.

12. *Environmental justice* affirms the need for urban and rural ecological policies to clean up and rebuild our cities and rural areas in balance with nature, honoring the cultural integrity of all our communities, and providing fair access for all to the full range of resources.

13. *Environmental justice* calls for the strict enforcement of principles of informed consent, and a halt to the testing of experimental reproductive and medical procedures and vaccinations on people of color.

14. *Environmental justice* opposes the destructive operations of multi-national corporations.

15. *Environmental justice* opposes military occupation, repression and exploitation of lands, peoples and cultures, and other life forms.

16. *Environmental justice* calls for the education of present and future generations which emphasizes social and environmental issues, based on our experience and an appreciation of our diverse cultural perspectives.

17. *Environmental justice* requires that we, as individuals, make personal and consumer choices to consume as little of Mother Earth's resources and to produce as little waste as possible; and make the conscious decision to challenge and reprioritize our lifestyles to insure the health of the natural world for present and future generations.

NOTES

Chapter 1

1. Robert D. Bullard, ed., *Unequal Protection: Environmental Justice and Communities of Color* (San Francisco: Sierra Club Books, 1994); Robert D. Bullard, ed., *Confronting Environmental Racism: Voices from the Grassroots* (Boston, Mass.: South End Press, 1993); Richard Hofrichter, ed., *Toxic Struggles: The Theory and Practice of Environmental Justice* (Philadelphia, Pennsylvania and Gabriola Island, British Columbia: New Society Publishers, 1993); Vernice D. Miller, "Planning, Power and Politics: A Case Study of the Land Use and Siting History of the North River Water Pollution Control Plant," *Fordham Urban Law Journal* 21 (Spring 1994): 707–22.

2. Chapter 2 discusses this large (and growing) literature more fully. Three recent examples of published empirical assessment by nonactivists include Ann O'M. Bowman and Kelley Crews-Meyer, "Locating Southern LULUs: Race, Class, and Environmental Justice," *State and Local Government Review* 29 (Spring 1997): 110–19; Vicki Been, "Analyzing Evidence of Environmental Justice," *Journal of Land Use & Environmental Law* 11 (Fall 1995): 1–36; and Brett Baden and Don Coursey, *The Locality of Waste Sites Within the City of Chicago: A Demographic, Social, and Economic Analysis*, Working Paper Series 97-2, Irving B. Harris Graduate School of Public Policy Studies, University of Chicago (1997).

3. In addition to the edited volumes *Unequal Protection* and *Confronting Environmental Racism*, see Robert D. Bullard, *Dumping in Dixie: Race, Class, and Environmental Quality* (Boulder, Colorado: Westview Press, 1990). Bullard's activist bent is perhaps most vividly displayed in the speech reprinted in United

Church of Christ, Commission for Racial Justice, "African American Historical and Cultural Perspectives on Environmental Justice," *Proceedings: The First National People of Color Environmental Leadership Summit* (October 24–27, 1991): 29–31.

4. Quoted in Andrew Szasz, *EcoPopulism: Toxic Waste and the Movement for Environmental Justice* (Minneapolis and London: University of Minnesota Press, 1994), p. 160. On this point see also Kenneth A. Gould, Allan Schnaiberg, and Adam S. Weinberg, *Local Environmental Struggles: Citizen Activism in the Treadmill of Production* (Cambridge, England: Cambridge University Press), p. 40.

5. John A. Hird, *Superfund: The Political Economy of Risk* (Baltimore and London: Johns Hopkins University Press, 1994).

6. Bruce A. Williams and Albert R. Matheny, *Democracy, Dialogue, and Environmental Disputes: The Contested Languages of Social Regulation* (New Haven and London: Yale University Press, 1995).

7. Howard Margolis, *Dealing with Risk: Why the Public and the Experts Disagree on Environmental Issues* (Chicago and London: University of Chicago Press, 1996).

8. For example, a document produced by the Louisiana Chemical Association (LCA) observes that "LCA polls show that the average Louisiana citizen does not trust the chemical industry and has a low opinion of our performance. Blacks and other minority citizens trust us even less." See Louisiana Advisory Committee to the U.S. Commission on Civil Rights, *The Battle for Environmental Justice in Louisiana . . . Government, Industry, and the People* (September, 1993), p. 110.

9. Szasz, *EcoPopulism.*

10. Marc K. Landy and Martin A. Levin, eds., *The New Politics of Public Policy* (Baltimore and London: Johns Hopkins University Press, 1995). See also Louisiana Advisory Committee, *The Battle for Environmental Justice in Louisiana*, p. 16.

11. Richard A. Harris and Sidney M. Milkis, *The Politics of Regulatory Change: A Tale of Two Agencies* (New York and Oxford: Oxford University Press, 1989).

12. On this point see Helen M. Ingram, David H. Colnic, and Dean E. Mann, "Interest Groups and Environmental Policy," in James P. Lester, ed., *Environmental Politics and Policy: Theories and Evidence*, 2nd ed. (Durham and London: Duke University Press, 1995), p. 120. For example, Richard Moore of the Southwest Network for Environmental and Economic Justice branded the Sierra Club a "co-conspirator in attempting to take away resources from our communities" and part of the environmental establishment that was "supporting policies that emphasize the cleanup and preservation of the environment on the backs of working people, and people of color in particular."

13. Luke W. Cole, "Remedies for Environmental Racism: A View from the Field," *Michigan Law Review* 90 (June 1992): 1995 (emphasis in the original).

Chapter 2

1. As one reporter observes regarding contests over the national political lexicon: "Whoever controls the language controls the debate. In an era when voters and politicians are afflicted with information overload, the short-hand description of a policy proposal necessarily colors the popular view of it. A single loaded word or two can cement a public impression that drastically alters the political dynamics." Peter Baker, "White House Finds 'Fast Track' Too Slippery," *Washington Post*, September 14, 1997, A4.

2. In offering his own definitions of these terms, scholar and environmental justice advocate Bunyan Bryant observes that "the literature is conspicuously without definitions" and that "these concepts mean different things to different people." See Bunyan Bryant, "Introduction," in Bunyan Bryant, ed., *Environmental Justice: Issues, Policies, and Solutions* (Washington, D.C.: Island Press, 1995), pp. 5–6.

3. On the politics of issue definition more generally see David A. Rochefort and Roger W. Cobb, eds., *The Politics of Problem Definition: Shaping the Policy Agenda* (Lawrence, Kansas: University Press of Kansas, 1994).

4. An exception is Peter S. Wenz, *Environmental Justice* (Albany: State University of New York Press, 1988).

5. Bryant, "Introduction," p. 5.

6. See Environmental Protection Agency, *Environmental Equity: Reducing Risk for All Communities*, vols. 1 and 2 (June 1992).

7. Ibid., vol. 2, p. 2.

8. James T. Hamilton, "Testing for Environmental Racism: Prejudice, Profits, Political Power?" *Journal of Policy Analysis and Management* 14 (Winter 1995): p. 129.

9. Speech reprinted in United Church of Christ, Commission for Racial Justice, "Historical Significance and Challenges of The First National People of Color Environmental Leadership Summit," *Proceedings: The First National People of Color Environmental Leadership Summit* (October 24–27, 1991), p. 8. On this point see also testimony by Pat Bryant, executive director of the Gulf Coast Tenants Association, U.S. Congress, House of Representatives, Committee on the Judiciary, "Environmental Justice" (hearings before the subcommittee on civil and constitutional rights), 103d Cong., 1st sess., March 3 and 4, 1993, p. 10.

10. Robert D. Bullard, *Dumping in Dixie: Race, Class, and Environmental Quality* (Boulder, Colorado: Westview Press, 1994), p. 98.

11. Attribution of the term to Chavis is offered in Charles Lee, "Toxic Waste and Race in the United States," in Bunyan Bryant and Paul Mohai, eds., *Race and the Incidence of Environmental Hazards: A Time for Discourse* (Boulder, Colo.: Westview Press, 1992), p. 10.

12. Shelby Steele, "The Race Not Run," *New Republic* October 7, 1996, p. 23. Moreover, many minority analysts and activists incline toward defining racism as "racial prejudice plus power." Since people of color are assumed to have little or no power, such a formulation has the convenient effect of shielding those activists and analysts against charges that they themselves may be racist. For this formulation see United Church of Christ, Commission for Racial Justice, *Toxic Wastes and Race in the United States: A National Report on the Racial and Socio-Economic Characteristics of Communities with Hazardous Waste Sites,* (New York: United Church of Christ, 1987) pp. ix–x.

13. Eugene Grigsby, "Don't Cry Wolf on Environmental Racism," *Los Angeles Times,* April 10, 1996, A11.

14. U.S. Environmental Protection Agency, Office of Enforcement and Compliance Assurance, Office of Environmental Justice, *Small Grants Program Application Guidance—FY 1997* (Washington, D.C., December 1996), p. 2.

15. The Principles of Environmental Justice are contained in United Church of Christ, *Proceedings,* pp. xiii–xiv.

16. *Environmental Justice* Hearings, pp. 10–15.

17. Bunyan Bryant's definition is indicative: "Environmental justice (EJ) is broader in scope than environmental equity. It refers to those cultural norms and values, rules, regulations, behaviors, policies, and decisions to support sustainable communities, where people can interact with confidence that their environment is safe, nurturing, and productive. Environmental justice is served when people can realize their highest potential, without experiencing the 'isms.' Environmental justice is supported by decent paying and safe jobs; quality schools and recreation; decent housing and adequate health care; democratic decision-making and personal empowerment; and communities free of violence, drugs, and poverty. These are communities where both cultural and biological diversity are respected and highly revered and where distributed justice prevails." (Bryant, p. 6)

18. See Ronald A. Foresta, *America's National Parks and Their Keepers* (Washington, D.C.: Resources for the Future, 1984).

19. A number of commentators have suggested that portrayal of minorities as unconcerned with environmental issues is inaccurate if one defines "the environment" as including concrete threats to human health. See Dorceta Taylor, "Can the Environmental Movement Attract and Maintain the Support of Minorities?" in Bryant and Mohai, eds., *Race and the Incidence of Environmental Hazards,* pp. 28–54.

20. On the nature of organizational incentives generally, and purposive incentives in particular, see James Q. Wilson, *Political Organizations,* updated ed. (Princeton, N.J.: Princeton University Press, 1995).

21. Nevertheless, national environmental organizations, such as the Sierra Club and the National Wildlife Federation, have begun to make room for envi-

ronmental justice concerns. By the mid-1990s, for example, environmental justice matters dominated the work of the Sierra Club Legal Defense Fund's New Orleans office. See Thom Weidlich, "Bias Suits Hit Activist Groups," *National Law Journal*, May 1, 1995, p. A1. Attacking political institutions for failing to perform functions they were not designed to perform is common in politics and can be an effective way of pressing for change in the target institutions. An example is the success of AIDS activists critical of the National Institutes of Health and the Food and Drug Administration. See Christopher H. Foreman Jr. "The Fast Track: Federal Agencies and the Political Demand for AIDS Drugs," *Brookings Review* 9 (Spring 1991): 30–37.

22. See John M. Ostheimer and Leonard G. Ritt, "Environment, Energy, and Black Americans," *Sage Research Papers in the Social Sciences* 4, series no. 90-025, Human Ecology subseries (Beverly Hills and London: 1976). For analysis of a later period see Henry Vance Davis, "The Environmental Voting Record of the Congressional Black Caucus," in Bryant and Mohai, eds., *Race and the Incidence of Environmental Hazards*, pp. 55–63.

23. Quoted in Walter A. Rosenbaum, *The Politics of Environmental Concern* (New York: Praeger, 1973), p. 74.

24. Quoted in Ostheimer and Ritt, "Environment, Energy, and Black Americans," p. 6.

25. Andrew Hurley, *Environmental Inequalities: Class, Race, and Industrial Pollution in Gary, Indiana, 1945–1980.* (Chapel Hill: University of North Carolina Press, 1995), ch. 5.

26. Mark E. Rushefsky, "Elites and Environmental Policy," in James P. Lester, ed., *Environmental Politics and Policy: Theories and Evidence,* 2nd ed. (Durham and London: Duke University Press, 1995), p. 284.

27. Aaron Wildavsky, *But Is It True? A Citizen's Guide to Environmental Health and Safety Issues* (Cambridge, Mass.: Harvard University Press, 1995), ch. 4 and Michael Fumento, *Science Under Siege: Balancing Technology and the Environment* (New York: William Morrow and Company, 1993), ch. 4.

28. On the EPA scandals of the early 1980s see Jonathan Lash, Katherine Gillman, and David Sheridan, *A Season of Spoils: The Reagan Administration's Attack on the Environment* (New York: Pantheon Books, 1984), and Bruce A. Williams and Albert R. Matheny, *Democracy, Dialogue, and Environmental Disputes: The Contested Languages of Social Regulation* (New Haven: Yale University Press, 1995), ch. 5.

29. Daniel Mazmanian and David Morrell, *Beyond Superfailure: America's Toxics Policy for the 1990s* (Boulder, Colo.: Westview Press, 1992), ch. 1.

30. Helen M. Ingram, David H. Colnic, and Dean E. Mann, "Interest Groups and Environmental Policy," in Lester, ed., *Environmental Politics and Policy,* pp. 119–21. Environmental anxieties have not been the sole spur to the creation of health-oriented grassroots groups. In a more general vein see Christopher H.

Foreman Jr., "Grassroots Victim Organizations: Mobilizing for Personal and Public Health," in Allan J. Cigler and Burdett A. Loomis, eds., *Interest Group Politics,* 4th ed. (Washington, D.C.: Congressional Quarterly Press, 1995), pp. 33–53.

31. Michael C. Dawson, *Behind the Mule: Race and Class in African-American Politics* (Princeton, N.J.: Princeton University Press, 1994).

32. Bullard, *Dumping in Dixie,* p. 29.

33. Luke W. Cole, "Environmental Justice Litigation: Another Stone in David's Sling," *Fordham Urban Law Journal* 21 (1994): 523. The case was brought by Linda McKeever Bullard, spouse of Robert Bullard.

34. The Warren County saga recurs often in the environmental justice literature. See Bullard, *Dumping in Dixie,* pp. 29–32; Ken Geiser and Gerry Waneck, "PCBs and Warren County," in Robert D. Bullard, ed., *Unequal Protection: Environmental Justice and Communities of Color* (San Francisco: Sierra Club Books, 1994), pp. 43–52; Charles Lee, "Toxic Waste and Race in the United States," in Bryant and Mohai, eds., *Race and the Incidence of Environmental Hazards,* p. 12; Charles Lee, "Beyond Toxic Wastes and Race," in Robert D. Bullard, ed., *Confronting Environmental Racism: Voices from the Grassroots* (Boston, Mass.: South End Press, 1993), p. 43; and Marc Mowrey and Tim Redmond, *Not in Our Backyard: The People and Events That Shaped America's Modern Environmental Movement* (New York: William Morrow, 1993), pp. 433–34.

35. Bullard, *Dumping in Dixie,* pp. 29–30.

36. Geiser and Waneck, "PCBs and Warren County," p. 52.

37. U.S. General Accounting Office, *Siting of Hazardous Waste Landfills and Their Correlation with Racial and Economic Status of Surrounding Communities* (GAO/RCED-83-168), June 1, 1983.

38. U.S. General Accounting Office, *Siting of Hazardous Waste Landfills,* p. 1.

39. This is known as the problem of aggregation. For a discussion of numerous methodological problems that bedevil environmental equity research see Kelley A. Crews-Meyer and Wayne R. Meyer, "Feasibility and Accuracy in Environmental Equity Research," paper presented to the 1996 annual meeting of the American Political Science Association.

40. See Vicki Been, "Locally Undesirable Land Uses in Minority Neighborhoods: Disproportionate Siting or Market Dynamics?" *Yale Law Journal* 103 (April 1994): 1406.

41. Hamilton, "Testing for Environmental Racism," p. 110.

42. See for example Robert D. Bullard, "Unequal Environmental Protection: Incorporating Environmental Justice in Decision Making," in Adam M. Finkel and Dominic Golding, eds., *Worst Things First? The Debate over Risk-Based National Environmental Priorities* (Washington, D.C.: Resources for the Future, 1994), pp. 237–66.

43. The full title of the study is United Church of Christ, Commission for Racial Justice, *Toxic Wastes and Race in the United States: A National Report on the Racial and Socio-Economic Characteristics of Communities with Hazardous Waste Sites.*

44. Ibid., p. xii.

45. Ibid., p. xiii.

46. Ibid., p. 13.

47. Crews-Meyer and Meyer, "Feasibility and Accuracy," p. 7.

48. See testimony of Charles J. McDermott, director of government affairs for Waste Management Inc., in *Environmental Justice Hearings*, p. 71–74; and Barry G. Rabe, *Beyond NIMBY: Hazardous Waste Siting in Canada and the United States* (Washington, D.C.: Brookings, 1994), p. 17.

49. Hamilton, "Testing for Environmental Racism," p. 107.

50. Paul Mohai and Bunyan Bryant, "Environmental Racism: Reviewing the Evidence," in Bryant and Mohai, eds., *Race and the Incidence of Environmental Hazards,* pp. 163–76.

51. Ibid, pp. 165–169.

52. Vicki Been, "Locally Undesirable Land Uses in Minority Neighborhoods: Disproportionate Siting or Market Dynamics?" *Yale Law Journal* 103 (April 1994): 1406.

53. Marianne Lavelle and Marcia Coyle, "Unequal Protection: The Racial Divide in Environmental Law," *National Law Journal* (September 21, 1992): S1–S6.

54. Ibid., p. S2.

55. Environmental Protection Agency, "Equity in the Enforcement of the Federal Environmental Laws: A Report to the EPA Enforcement Management Council by the EMC Workgroup on Equity in Enforcement," undated unpublished report, p. 81.

56. Mark Atlas, "The Contaminated Grassy Knoll: Searching for Environmental Justice Conspiracies in Environmental Enforcement," paper presented to Association for Public Policy Analysis and Management Conference, November 6, 1997, p. 8.

57. Atlas, "The Contaminated Grassy Knoll," p. 26.

58. Douglas L. Anderton, "Hazardous Waste Facilities: 'Environmental Equity' Issues in Metropolitan Areas," *Evaluation Review* 18 (April 1994): 123. See also Andy B. Anderson, Douglas L. Anderton, and John Michael Oakes, "Environmental Equity: Evaluating TSDF Siting Over the Past Two Decades," *Waste Age* (July 1994): 83–84, 86, 88, 90, 92, 94, 96, 98, 100.

59. John A. Hird, *Superfund: The Political Economy of Environmental Risk* (Baltimore and London: Johns Hopkins University Press, 1994), p. 136.

60. As John Hird observes: "Only those sites scoring over 28.5 on a 100-point [hazard assessment] scale are eligible for listing on the NPL. . . . The choice of

28.5 as the cutoff score was an arbitrary one, meant simply to ensure that the initial congressionally mandated minimum of four hundred sites would be included on the initial NPL. This particular choice of cutoff is particularly important, however, since it defines whether or not future sites will qualify for the NPL" (Hird, *Superfund*, p. 108).

61. Brett Baden and Don Coursey, "The Locality of Waste Sites Within the City of Chicago: A Demographic, Social, and Economic Analysis" Working Paper Series 97-2 (Chicago: University of Chicago, 1997), p. 40.

62. General Accounting Office, *Hazardous and Nonhazardous Waste: Demographics of People Living Near Waste Facilities* (GAO/RCED-95-84), June 1995, p. 20.

63. Ann O'M. Bowman and Kelley A. Crews-Meyer, "Locating Southern LULUs: Race, Class, and Environmental Justice," *State and Local Government Review* 29 (Spring 1997): 110–19.

64. Ibid., p. 114.

65. Ibid., p. 116.

66. See Christopher Boerner and Thomas Lambert, *Environmental Justice?* Policy Study Number 121 (St. Louis: Center for the Study of American Business, April 1994): 4–6, and Thomas Lambert and Christopher Boerner, *Environmental Inequity: Economic Causes, Economic Solutions* Policy Study Number 125 (St. Louis: Center for the Study of American Business, June 1995): 3–7.

67. Vicki Been, "What's Fairness Got to Do With It? Environmental Justice and the Siting of Locally Undesirable Land Uses," *Cornell Law Review* 78 (1993): 1003.

68. See Bryant, "Introduction," in Bryant, pp. 1–7.

69. Howard Margolis, *Dealing with Risk: Why the Public and the Experts Disagree on Environmental Issues* (Chicago: University of Chicago Press, 1996). See also Michael Specter, "Seeing Risk Everywhere: In Epidemic of Fear, Major Threats Ignored," *Washington Post*, May 7, 1989, A1.

70. Bryant and Mohai, "Introduction," in Bryant and Mohai, eds., *Race and the Incidence of Environmental Hazards*, p. 5.

71 Bullard, *Dumping in Dixie*, p. 115.

72 The bill was reintroduced in 1993 by Representative Lewis and Senator Max Baucus (D-Montana). See U.S. Congress, House of Representatives, Committee on Energy and Commerce, *Environmental Issues* (Hearings before the Subcommittee on Transportation and Hazardous Materials), 103d Cong., 1st sess., (November 17-18, 1993), pp. 134–46.

73. Ibid., pp. 123–31.

74. Andrew M. Ballard et al., "Property Rights Measure Most Visible of Several Proposals to Curb Regulation," Bureau of National Affairs, *Environment Reporter* (April 20, 1995): 2502–06. See also Charles C. Mann and Mark L.

Plummer, "Environmental Law Is Wrecking the Environment," *New York Times,* March 2, 1995, A23.

75. See Environmental Justice Project, Lawyers' Committee for Civil Rights Under Law, "Recommendations to the Presidential Transition Team for the U.S. Environmental Protection Agency on Environmental Justice Issues Submitted by the Environmental Justice Transition Group," December 21, 1992.

76. Ibid., p. 3.

77. Ibid.

78. Ibid., p. 4.

79. Ibid.

80. On the changes made in the executive order see Memorandum to Office of Environmental Justice Staff from Marty Halper, February 17, 1994. See also Gary Lee, "EPA-Clinton Executive Order Gives Boost to Mission," *Washington Post,* February 17, 1994, p. A21.

81. "Executive Order 12898-Federal Actions to Address Environmental Justice in Minority Populations and Low-Income Populations," *Weekly Compilation of Presidential Documents,* vol. 30 (February 14, 1994), p. 276.

Chapter 3

1. "Furthering the Principles of Environmental Justice," paper prepared by the Policy Conference on Environmental Justice, Woodrow Wilson School of Public and International Affairs, Princeton University, January 10, 1995, p. 9.

2. John Clayton Thomas, *Public Participation in Public Decisions: New Skills and Strategies for Public Managers* (San Francisco: Jossey-Bass, 1995), ch. 2. See also Daniel P. Moynihan, *Maximum Feasible Misunderstanding: Community Action in the War on Poverty* (New York: Free Press, 1970) and the critique of Moynihan's analysis in Jeffrey M. Berry, Kent E. Portney, and Ken Thomson, *The Rebirth of Urban Democracy* (Washington, D.C.: Brookings Institution, 1993), pp. 22–30.

3. Toddi A Steelman. and William Ascher observe that "public input can be envisioned as playing a role in the intelligence function" for agencies, a way of providing data for the policymaker. But it can also be construed as "part of the process of the authoritative selection of policies: their prescription, invocation, and application." They note that "confusion results when public input is solicited by bureaucrats without much regard for the function it is to play in developing policy." See Toddi A. Steelman and William Ascher "Public Involvement Methods in Natural Resource Policy Making: Advantages, Disadvantages and Trade-offs," *Policy Sciences* 30 (May 1997): 74.

4. *Weekly Compilation of Presidential Documents,* vol. 30 (February 14, 1994), pp. 278–79.

5. "Executive Order 12898-Federal Actions to Address Environmental Justice in Minority Populations and Low-Income Populations." "Memorandum on Environmental Justice." *Weekly Compilation of Presidential Documents*, vol. 30 (February 14, 1994).

6. Ibid., p. 280.

7. Quoted in Office of Environmental Justice, *Environmental Justice Strategy: Executive Order 12898* (Washington, D.C.: Environmental Protection Agency, April 1995), p. 2.

8. James A. Morone, *The Democratic Wish: Popular Participation and the Limits of American Government* (New York: Basic Books, 1990), p. 5.

9. The following remarks are contained in *Meeting Summary of the Executive Council of the National Environmental Justice Advisory Council—January 17–19, 1995, Atlanta, Georgia*, pp. 25–32.

10. Emphasis added to the final two sentences. Herrera's remarks came in response to a speaker during the public comment period who directed hostile comments toward the NEJAC.

11. Christopher H. Foreman Jr., *Plagues, Products and Politics: Emergent Public Health Hazards and National Policymaking* (Washington, D.C.: Brookings Institution, 1994), esp. ch. 3.

12. On emergency removals see: Thomas W. Church and Robert T. Nakamura, *Cleaning Up the Mess: Implementation Strategies in Superfund* (Washington, D.C.: Brookings Institution, 1993), pp. 5–6; Aaron Wildavsky and David Schleicher, "Superfund's Abandoned Hazardous Waste Sites," in Aaron Wildavsky, *But Is It True? A Citizen's Guide to Environmental Health and Safety Issues* (Cambridge, Mass.: Harvard University Press, 1995), p. 156; and Daniel Mazmanian and David Morell, *Beyond Superfailure: America's Toxics Policy for the 1990s* (Boulder, Colo.: Westview Press, 1992), p. 34.

13. For example, analysis of the potential and likely impacts of a given chemical on public health may be so uncertain that "government officials are reluctant to advise citizens about whether or not they should take precautions. Citizens interpret this government hesitation as 'stonewalling.'" Mazmanian and Morell, p. 71.

14. Howard Margolis, *Dealing with Risk: Why the Public and the Experts Disagree on Environmental Issues* (Chicago: University of Chicago Press, 1996).

15. Heather M. Little, "Toxin Shock: Husband's Death from Cancer Set Off Her Environmental War," *Chicago Tribune*, January 15, 1995, Section Womanews, p. 3.

16. Hazel Johnson, "Surviving in Chicago's 'Toxic Doughnut,'" in Robert D. Bullard, *People of Color Environmental Groups—1994–95 Directory* (Atlanta: Environmental Justice Resource Center, Clark Atlanta University, 1994), p. 17.

17. Benjamin A. Goldman, *The Truth About Where You Live: An Atlas for Action on Toxins and Mortality* (New York: Random House, 1991), p. 23.

18. On the politics of community right-to-know, and the Toxics Release Inventory in particular, see Robert Gottlieb, Maureen Smith, Julie Roque, and Pamela Yates, "New Approaches to Toxics: Production Design, Right-to-Know, and Definition Debates," in Robert Gottlieb, ed., *Reducing Toxics: A New Approach to Policy and Industrial Decisionmaking* (Washington, D.C. and Covelo, Calf.: Island Press, 1995), pp. 124–65.

19. See Jeffrey M. Berry, Kent E. Portney, and Ken Thomson, *The Rebirth of Urban Democracy* (Washington, D.C.: Brookings Institution, 1993), ch. 2.

20. Barry G. Rabe, *Beyond NIMBY: Hazardous Waste Siting in Canada and the United States* (Washington, D.C.: Brookings Institution, 1994). See also Mazmanian and Morell, ch. 7.

21. Vernice D. Miller, "Planning, Power and Politics: A Case Study of the Land Use and Siting History of the North River Water Pollution Control Plant," *Fordham Urban Law Journal* 21 (Spring 1994): 721.

22. Ken Geiser and Garry Waneck, "PCBs and Warren County," in Robert D. Bullard, ed., *Unequal Protection: Environmental Justice and Communities of Color* (San Francisco: Sierra Club Books, 1994), p. 52.

23. Louisiana Advisory Committee to the U.S. Commission on Civil Rights, *The Battle for Environmental Justice in Louisiana . . . Government Industry, and the People* (September 1993), pp. 46–62.

24. Indeed the permit was effectively fended off for several years and in April 1992 LES ultimately gave up its quest to operate the Claiborne Enrichment Center. See "Federal Implementation of Environmental Justice Policies" *LLW notes* (Washington D.C.: LLW Forum c/o Afton Associates, April 1998), p. 3.

25. On this point see the dissent by member John S. Baker Jr., in Louisiana Advisory Committee to the U.S. Commission on Civil Rights, pp. 69–72.

26. Michael Janofsky, "Suit Says Racial Bias Led to Clustering of Solid-Waste Sites," *New York Times*, May 29, 1996, p. A15.

27. John Clayton Thomas, *Public Participation in Public Decisions: New Skills and Strategies for Public Managers* (San Francisco: Jossey-Bass, 1995), p. 25.

28. See Raymond E. Wolfinger and Steven J. Rosenstone, *Who Votes?* (New Haven: Yale University Press, 1980). See also Sidney Verba and Norman H. Nie, *Participation in America: Political Democracy and Social Equality* (New York: Harper and Row, 1972), pp. 97–101.

29. See Symposium on Health Research and Needs to Ensure Environmental Justice, *Executive Summary and Proceedings*, (Arlington, VA; February 10–12, 1994). See also Sylvia N. Tesh and Bruce A. Williams, "Identity Politics, Disinterested Politics and Environmental Justice." *Polity*, vol. 28 (Spring 1996), p. 297.

30. Interview with an EPA official.

31. Richard L. Cole and David A. Caputo, "The Public Hearing as an Effective Citizen Participation Mechanism: A Case Study of the General Revenue Sharing Program," *American Political Science Review* 78 (June 1984): 404–16.

32. On this point see Christopher H. Foreman Jr. "Grassroots Victim Organizations: Mobilizing for Personal and Public Health," in Allan J. Cigler and Burdett A. Loomis, eds., *Interest Group Politics*, 4th ed. (Washington, D.C.: Congressional Quarterly Press, 1995), pp. 33–53.

33. Marilyn Gittell and others, *Limits to Citizen Participation: The Decline of Community Organizations* (Beverly Hills: Sage Publications, 1980), ch. 2.

34. Office of Environmental Justice, *Environmental Justice 1994 Annual Report* (Washington, D.C.: Environmental Protection Agency, April 1995), p. 3.

35. The charter, approved July 23, 1993, is contained in the appendix to *Proceedings of the National Environmental Justice Advisory Council Meeting, May 20, 1994.*

36. Letter dated May 11, 1994, to Carol Browner from the Alliance for the Washington Office on Environmental Justice, in ibid.

37. Interview with NEJAC member.

38. National Environmental Justice Advisory Council, *The Model Plan for Public Participation,* (Washington, D.C.: Environmental Protection Agency, November 1996), p. i.

39. National Environmental Justice Advisory Council, *Summary of the Meeting of the National Environmental Justice Advisory Council,* Washington, D.C., December 12–14, 1995, p. ES-5.

40. For a discussion of review committees like these Foreman Jr. *Plagues, Products and Politics.* See also Dorothy Nelkin, "Science and Technology Policy and the Democratic Process," in James C. Petersen, ed., *Citizen Participation in Science Policy* (Amherst: University of Massachusetts Press, 1984), pp. 18–39.

41. See Council on Environmental Quality, "Draft Guidance for Addressing Environmental Justice under The National Environmental Policy Act," (Washington, D.C.: CEQ, May 24, 1996); Nuclear Regulatory Commission, "Draft Strategic Plan: Environmental Justice," (1995) and EPA, "Draft Environmental Justice Strategy for Executive Order 12898." (January 1995).

42. Interview with NEJAC member.

43. House of Representatives, Committee on Appropriations, *Departments of Veterans Affairs and Housing and Urban Development, and Independent Agencies Appropriations for 1997* (hearings before a subcommittee), 104th Cong., 2 sess., (GPO: April 16, 1996), p. 211.

44. See National Environmental Justice Advisory Council, *Summary of the Meeting of the National Environmental Justice Advisory Council,* Baltimore, Md., December 10–12, 1996, pp. 2–4.

45. See Joel A. Mintz, *Enforcement at the EPA: High Stakes and Hard Choices* (Austin: University of Texas Press, 1995), ch. 2 and Marc K. Landy, Marc J. Roberts, and Stephen R. Thomas, *The Environmental Protection Agency: Asking the Wrong Questions: From Nixon to Clinton,* expanded ed. (New York and Oxford: Oxford University Press, 1994), ch. 7.

46. National Environmental Justice Advisory Council, *Summary of the Meeting of the National Environmental Justice Advisory Council*, Washington, D.C., July 25–26, 1995, p. 27.

47. Ibid., p. 28.

48. Ibid., pp. 30–31.

49. Office of Environmental Justice, *Community/University Partnership Grants Program Application Guidance—FY 1997* (Washington, D.C.: Environmental Protection Agency, December 1996).

50. National Environmental Justice Advisory Council, *Summary of the Meeting of the National Environmental Justice Advisory Council—Executive Summary*, Durham, North Carolina, December 8–10, 1997, p. ES-2.

51. U.S. Environmental Protection Agency, Office of Enforcement and Compliance Assurance, Office of Environmental Justice, *Small Grants Program Application Guidance—FY 1997* (Washington, D.C.: December 1996), p. 2.

52. *Summary of the Meeting of the National Environmental Justice Advisory Council*, p. 31.

53. "Historically, when the U.S. Environmental Protection Agency took a civil administrative action against a violating facility, it sought only monetary penalties. In the 1990s, however, EPA changed its enforcement approach to seek not only monetary penalties but also an improvement in environmental quality. Environmental improvement is expected to occur as a result of Supplemental Environmental Projects (SEPs). A SEP is a project that a respondent/defendant in a case agrees to conduct as a term of settlement sometimes in exchange for partial mitigation of a civil penalty." Office of Enforcement and Compliance Assurance, *Enforcement and Compliance Assurance Accomplishments Report—FY 1994* (Washington, D.C.: Environmental Protection Agency, May 1995), pp. 2–12.

54. Author's notes.

55. Environmental Protection Agency, *Environmental Justice, Urban Revitalization, and Brownfields: The Search for Authentic Signs of Hope—A Report on the Public Dialogues on Urban Revitalization and Brownfields: Envisioning Healthy and Sustainable Communities* (December 1996).

56. Charles Bartsch and Elizabeth Collaton, *Coming Clean for Economic Development: A Resource Book on Environmental Cleanup and Economic Development Opportunities* (Washington, D.C.: Northeast-Midwest Institute, September 1996), p. 38.

57. Department of the Interior, *Department of the Interior Strategic Plan: Environmental Justice*, January 1995, p. 2.

58. Ibid., p. 2, emphasis added.

59. Ibid., pp. 7, 18.

60. Department of Defense, *Department of Defense Strategy on Environmental Justice* (Washington, D.C.: March 24, 1995), p. 5.

61. Ibid., p. 4.

62. Memo from Jennifer L. Pennell to the author, November 20, 1995, on discussions with Ken Kumor of NASA regarding environmental justice strategies and implementation. On file with the author.

63. Regulations issued by the Council on Environmental Quality define "scoping" as "an early and open process for determining the scope of issues to be addressed and for identifying the significant issues related to a proposed action." 40 *Code of Federal Regulations* 1501.7.

64. Memo from Jennifer L. Pennell to the author, October 11, 1995, on a meeting with Maria Lopez-Otin, office of state programs at the Nuclear Regulatory Commission. On file with the author.

65. On Title VI of the Civil Rights Act see Richard J. Lazarus, "Pursuing 'Environmental Justice': The Distributional Effects of Environmental Protection," *Northwestern University Law Review* 87 (1993): 834–39. There has been discussion of Title VIII of the Civil Rights Act of 1968 and 42 U.S.C. section 1982 as potential environmental justice levers but as these are not currently the focus I do not deal with them here. See Lazarus, "Pursuing 'Environmental Justice,'" pp. 839–42.

66. *Weekly Compilation of Presidential Documents* 30, February 14, 1994, p. 279.

67. Section One of the Fourteenth Amendment to the United States Constitution, ratified in 1868, reads in part: "[No state shall]. . . . deny to any person within its jurisdiction the equal protection of the laws." On Title VI see: Luke W. Cole, "Environmental Justice Litigation: Another Stone in David's Sling," *Fordham Urban Law Journal* 21 (Spring 1994): 523–45; Lazarus, pp. 787–857; and James H. Colopy, "The Road Less Traveled: Pursuing Environmental Justice Through Title VI of the Civil Rights Act of 1964," *Stanford Environmental Law Journal* 13 (1994): 125–89.

68. The key cases are *Washington v. Davis* 426 U.S. 229, (1976) and *Arlington Heights v. Metropolitan Housing Development Corp.* 429 U.S. 252 (1977).

69. Colopy, "The Road Less Traveled," p. 146.

70. Lazarus, "Pursuing 'Environmental Justice,'" p. 834.

71. Ibid., p. 836.

72. Ibid.

73. Ibid., p. 835.

74. For a summary of a NEJAC briefing on Title VI by Rodney Cash, associate director of the discrimination complaints and external compliance staff of OCR, see National Environmental Justice Advisory Council, *Summary of the Meeting of the National Environmental Justice Advisory Council—Detroit Michigan,* May 29–30, 1996, pp. 2-14–2-16. Typed lists identifying and summarizing complaints as rejected/dismissed and those under consideration/investigation were distributed at the meeting and are in the author's files.

75. *Chester Residents v. Seif* 132 F.3d 925 (3rd Cir. 1997).

76. Cole, "Environmental Justice Litigation," pp. 532–33.

77. See Cole, "Environmental Justice Litigation," esp. pp. 541–45 and Luke W. Cole, "Remedies for Environmental Racism: A View from the Field," *Michigan Law Review* 90 (June 1992): 1991–97.

78. Cole, "Environmental Justice Litigation," pp. 541–42.

79. Richard N.L. Andrews, *NEPA in the Courts.*

80. In March 1998, the Environmental Council of the States (ECOS), a group representing state environmental authorities, condemned the interim guidance in a strongly worded resolution. See ECOS resolution number 98-2 titled "Environmental Protection Agency's Interim Guidance for Investigating Environmental Permit Challenges," approved March 26, 1998, in New Orleans, Louisiana. See also John H. Cushman Jr., "Pollution Policy Is Unfair Burden, States Tell E.P.A.," *New York Times*, May 10, 1998, p. A1.

81. Glenn Elasser, "Supreme Court to Hear Waste-Site Racism Case," *Chicago Tribune*, June 9, 1998.

82. Richard N.L. Andrews, *NEPA in the Courts.*

83. Cole, "Environmental Justice Litigation," pp. 526–27.

84. "Each Federal agency shall analyze the environmental effects, including human health, economic and social effects, of Federal actions including effects on minority communities, and low-income communities when such analysis is required by the National Environmental Policy Act of 1969 (NEPA), 42 U.S.C. section 4321 *et seq.*" "Memorandum on Environmental Justice," *Weekly Compilation of Presidential Documents* 30 (February 14, 1994), p. 280.

85. Council on Environmental Quality, *Draft Guidance for Addressing Environmental Justice under the National Environmental Policy Act*, Washington, D.C., May 24, 1996.

86. Letter to Richard Moore, Southwest Network for Environmental and Economic Justice from Bradley M. Campbell, associate director, Council on Environmental Quality, May 25, 1996.

87. Council on Environmental Quality, *Draft Guidance*, pp. 5–6.

88. Ibid., p. 7.

89. Ibid.

90. Office of Federal Activities, *Guidance for Incorporating Environmental Justice Concerns in EPA's NEPA Compliance Analyses* (Washington, D.C.: Environmental Protection Agency, July 12, 1996).

91. On Truman's desegregation order and the resistance to it, see Bernard C. Nalty, *Strength for the Fight: A History of Black Americans in the Military* (New York: The Free Press, 1986) chap 15. On opposition to the Reagan-Bush regulatory relief efforts see Christopher H. Foreman Jr., "Legislators, Regulators, and the OMB: The Congressional Challenge to Presidential Regulatory Relief," in

James A. Thurber, ed., *Divided Democracy: Cooperation and Conflict Between the President and Congress* (Washington, D.C.: Congressional Quarterly Press, 1991), pp. 123–43.

92. "Federal Consumer Programs," *Public Papers of the Presidents of the United States, Jimmy Carter, 1979*, (GPO: 1980), pp. 1762–66.

93. Ibid., p. 1763.

94. Louise G. Trubek, David M. Trubek, and Paul G. Kent, *The Executive Order on Consumer Affairs Programs: New Voice for "Consumers" in Federal Agencies?"* (Madison, Wisconsin: Center for Public Representation, April 15, 1980).

95. Laurie Goodstein, "Religious Leaders Join Forces to Fight Pollution in Poor Areas," *Washington Post*, February 7, 1997, p. A3.

Chapter 4

1. Reference to poisoning is sometimes explicit. See, for example, the testimony of Pat Bryant, executive director of the Gulf Coast Tenants Association, in House of Representatives, Committee on the Judiciary, *Environmental Justice* (Hearings before the Subcommittee on Civil and Constitutional Rights). 103d Cong., 1st sess., March 3 and 4, 1993, p. 9.

2. Thomas Lambert and Christopher Boerner, "Environmental Inequality: Economic Causes, Economic Solutions," *Yale Journal on Regulation* 14 (Winter 1997): 212–13.

3. The terms *regulatory* and *epidemiologic* as used here are not intended to describe opposing views on the cause of disease or fundamentally incompatible public health tools. These terms indicate contrasting engines of agenda- and priority-setting. Regulators often (though some would argue, insufficiently) employ epidemiological evidence in formulating policies. Nor is there anything about the discipline of epidemiology that places it in opposition to regulation.

4. Quoted in Joseph G. Morone and Edward J. Woodhouse, *Averting Catastrophe: Strategies for Regulating Risky Technologies* (Berkeley and Los Angeles: University of California Press, 1986), p. 24.

5. Lester B. Lave, *The Strategy of Social Regulation: Decision Frameworks for Policy* (Washington, D.C.: Brookings Institution, 1981), pp. 13 and 125.

6. The former kind of epidemiologic analysis is the case-control or retrospective study. The latter is the cohort, or prospective, study. For a clear and authoritative treatment of these two kinds of epidemiologic analysis see Marcia Angell, *Science on Trial: The Clash of Medical Evidence and the Law in the Breast Implant Case* (New York and London: W. W. Norton, 1996), ch. 5.

7. Christopher H. Foreman Jr., *Plagues, Products and Politics: Emergent Public Health Hazards and National Policymaking* (Washington, D.C.: Brookings Institution, 1994), ch. 3.

8. See, for example, Committee on Environmental Epidemiology, National Research Council, *Environmental Epidemiology: Volume 1—Public Health and Hazardous Wastes* (Washington, D.C.: National Academy Press, 1991), ch. 1.

9. For more on such organizations see Christopher H. Foreman Jr., "Grassroots Victim Organizations: Mobilizing for Personal and Public Health," in Allan J. Cigler and Burdett A. Loomis, eds., *Interest Group Politics*, 4th ed. (Washington, D.C.: Congressional Quarterly Press, 1995), pp. 33–53.

10. Michael Fumento, *Science Under Siege: Balancing Technology and the Environment* (New York: William Morrow and Company, 1993), and Aaron Wildavsky, *But Is It True? A Citizen's Guide to Environmental Health and Safety Issues* (Cambridge, Mass.: Harvard University Press, 1995). An overview of grassroots groups is Foreman, "Grassroots Victim Organizations," pp. 33–53. On Gulf War syndrome see Eric Schmitt, "No Proof, but New Clues on Gulf War Illness," *New York Times*, January 12, 1997, pp. D2, and David Brown, "The Gulf between 'Syndrome' and Poison Gas," *Washington Post*, January 2, 1997, pp. A1, A10.

11. James C. Robinson, *Toil and Toxics: Workplace Struggles and Political Strategies for Occupational Health* (Berkeley and Los Angeles, University of California Press, 1991), pp. xiii–xx. See also John Froines, Robert Gottlieb, Maureen Smith, and Pamela Yates, "Disassociating Toxics Policies: Occupational Risk and Product Hazards," in Robert Gottlieb, ed., *Reducing Toxics: A New Approach to Policy and Industrial Decisionmaking* (Washington, D.C.: Island Press, 1995), pp. 96–97.

12. Centers for Disease Control, "Guidelines for Investigating Clusters of Health Events," *Morbidity and Mortality Weekly Report—Recommendations and Reports* 39 (July 27, 1990): 2. See also Richard J. Waxweiler, William Stringer, Joseph K. Wagoner, and James Jones, "Neoplastic Risk Among Workers Exposed to Vinyl Chloride," *Annals of the New York Academy of Sciences* 271 (1976): 40–48, and Shanklin B. Cannon, et al., "Epidemic Kepone Poisoning in Chemical Workers," *American Journal of Epidemiology* 107 (1978): 529–37.

13. Centers for Disease Control, "Lead Poisoning Among Sandblasting Workers," *Morbidity and Mortality Weekly Report* 44 (January 27, 1995): 44. This issue of the *MMWR* reports on a Texas worker who presented at a hospital emergency room with a blood lead level of 111 micrograms/deciliter. The patient's symptoms included "abdominal pain, vomiting, weight loss, constipation, headache, memory loss, tinnitus, metallic taste in mouth, stuttering, arthralgias, and discoloration of the gums."

14. Centers for Disease Control, "Controlling Lead Toxicity in Bridge Workers," *Morbidity and Mortality Weekly Report* 44 (February 3, 1995): 78.

15. Robinson, *Toil and Toxics*, p. 127.

16. Ibid.

17. Michael Fumento, *Science Under Siege: Balancing Technology and the Environment* (New York: William Morrow and Co., 1993), pp. 109–113.

18. Lester B. Lave, "Clean Air Sense," *The Brookings Review* 15 (Summer 1997): 44.

19. Foreman, *Plagues, Products and Politics,* ch. 3.

20. Centers for Disease Control, "Guidelines for Investigating Clusters of Health Events," p. 3.

21. See Ross C. Brownson, Patrick L. Remington, and James R. Davis, eds., *Chronic Disease Epidemiology and Control* (Washington, D.C.: American Public Health Association, 1993), p. 45.

22. Ibid.

23. Alan C. Fisher, Wendy Worth, and Debra A. Mayer, *Update: Is There a Cancer Epidemic in the United States?* (New York: American Council on Science and Health, 1995). See also S. S. Devesa et al., "Recent Cancer Trends in the United States," *Journal of the National Cancer Institute* 87 (1994): 175–82.

24. Richard Doll and Richard Peto, *The Causes of Cancer* (New York and Oxford: Oxford University Press 1981). As Michael Gough has written: "Doll and Peto's decision to rely on human data has been criticized for a number of reasons. For one thing, epidemiology cannot identify small additional disease burdens; a negative epidemiologic study, even when many people are studied, can miss a 20 percent increase in cancer. The summation of many smaller increases—each undetectable by epidemiologic methods—could have a major impact on cancer rates, and Doll's and Peto's analysis might have overlooked them. Moreover, because many years may elapse between exposures and cancer manifestation, it can be argued that analysis of epidemiologic data can detect only the effects of exposures that occurred many years previously and could not possibly reveal effects of recent exposures." The main point of Gough's argument is that the findings of the Doll-Peto epidemiological approach actually jibe well with those of the toxicology-based risk assessment employed by the EPA. See Michael Gough, "Estimating Cancer Mortality," *Environmental Science and Technology* 23 (1989): 925–30; the quotation is from page 929.

25. United States Department of Health and Human Services, Public Health Service, *Healthy People 2000: Midcourse Review and 1995 Revisions* (Rockville, MD: US Public Health Service, 1996), p. 36.

26. Ibid.

27. Centers for Disease Control, "Cigarette Smoking Among American Indians and Alaskan Natives," *Morbidity and Mortality Weekly Report* 41 (November 13, 1992): 861.

28. Ibid.

29. Centers for Disease Control, "Cigarette Smoking Among Adults," *Morbidity and Mortality Weekly Report* 45 (July 12, 1996): 589. The CDC counsels

that the estimate for American Indian/Alaskan Native men should be interpreted caution because of the sample sizes used.

30. Ibid.

31. Beverly H. Wright, Pat Bryant, and Robert D. Bullard, "Coping with Poisons in Cancer Alley," in Robert D. Bullard, ed., *Unequal Protection: Environmental Justice and Communities of Color* (San Francisco: Sierra Club Books, 1994), pp. 110–29.

32. *Environmental Justice,* hearings, pp. 10–11.

33. Fumento, *Science Under Siege,* p. 83.

34. Fisher, Worth, and Meyer, p. 16.

35. See Marise S. Gottlieb, Charles L. Shear, and Daniel B. Seale, "Lung Cancer Mortality and Residential Proximity to Industry," *Environmental Health Perspectives* 45 (November 1982): 157–64. A study of lung cancer variation in the city of Philadelphia concluded that, while some data could be adduced to suggest air pollution as a causal factor in lung cancer incidence, "interpretation of a cause-and-effect relationship is unjustified because other important factors have not been taken into account. Smoking and occupational exposure are the most significant of these." See William Weiss, "Lung Cancer Mortality and Urban Air Pollution," *American Journal of Public Health* 68 (August 1978): 773–75; the quotation is from p. 775.

36. Otto Wong and Donna E. Foliart, "Epidemiological Factors of Cancer in Louisiana," *Journal of Environmental Pathology, Toxicology and Oncology* 12 (October 1993): 171–83; Benjamin F. Withers III, Paul W. Ferguson, and Douglas A. Swift, "Chemicals, Cancer, and Risk Assessment," *Journal of the Louisiana State Medical Society* 143 (January 1991): 33–40; Frank D. Groves, et al., "Is There a 'Cancer Corridor' in Louisiana?" *Journal of the Louisiana State Medical Society* 148 (April 1996): 155–65. Groves and his colleagues report: "Significantly lower (p<0.0001) incidence rates were found in South Louisiana among white females, black males, and black females for cancers of all sites combined; among women of both races for cancer of the breast; among men of both races for cancers of the colon and prostate; and among whites of both sexes for melanoma and rectal cancer. South Louisiana incidence rates were significantly higher than the [comparison national data generated by the National Cancer Institute] only for lung and larynx cancers in white males. The excess of lung cancer was statistically significant in four out of five regions [of South Louisiana] while the laryngeal cancer excess was significant only in the New Orleans area" (p. 155).

37. Groves, et al., "Is There a 'Cancer Corridor' in Louisiana?"

38. Lois Marie Gibbs and the Citizens Clearinghouse for Hazardous Waste, *Dying from Dioxin: A Citizen's Guide to Reclaiming Our Health and Rebuilding Democracy* (Boston: South End Press, 1995), and Ron Nixon, "There's Something in the H$_2$O," *YSB* (April 1996): 58–61, 65. See also the Greenpeace

bulletin entitled "PVC: The Poison Plastic," available from Greenpeace, Washington, D.C.

39. See Fumento, *Science Under Siege*, ch. 4, and Michael Gough, "Dioxin: Perceptions, Estimates, and Measures," in Kenneth R. Foster, David E. Bernstein, and Peter W. Huber, eds., *Phantom Risk: Scientific Inference and the Law* (Cambridge, Mass.: MIT Press, 1993), pp. 249–77.

40. Gough, "Dioxin: Perceptions, Estimates, and Measures," p. 251.

41. Fumento, *Science Under Siege*, chs. 4 and 5. See also Aaron Wildavsky with Brendon Swedlow, "Dioxin, Agent Orange, and Times Beach," in Aaron Wildavsky, *But It True? A Citizen's Guide to Environmental Health and Safety Issues* (Cambridge, Mass.: Harvard University Press, 1995), pp. 81–125.

42. International Agency for Research on Cancer, "IARC Evaluates Carcinogenic Risk Associated with Dioxins," press release issued February 14, 1997 (available at *www.iarc.fr/preleases/115e.htm*).

43. For an authoritative criticism of this approach see Bruce N. Ames and Lois Swirksy Gold, "Environmental Pollution and Cancer: Some Misconceptions," in Foster, Bernstein, and Huber, eds., *Phantom Risk*, pp. 153–57.

44. Theo Colborn, Dianne Dumanoski, and John Peterson Myers, *Our Stolen Future: Are We Threatening Our Fertility, Intelligence, and Survival?—A Scientific Detective Story* (New York: Dutton, 1996).

45. Ronald Bailey, "Hormones and Humbug," *Washington Post*, March 31, 1996, p. C3. See also Elizabeth M. Whelan, William M. London, and Leonard T. Flynn, *ACSH Commentary on Our Stolen Future* (New York: American Council on Science and Health, 1996).

46. Steven F. Arnold et al., "Synergistic Activation of Estrogen Receptor with Combinations of Environmental Chemicals," *Science* 272 (June 7, 1996): 1489–92. This study received considerable press attention. See Curt Suplee, "'Environmental Estrogens' May Pose Greater Risk, Study Shows," *Washington Post*, June 7, 1996, p. A4.

47. John A. McLachlan, "Synergistic Effect of Environmental Estrogens: Report Withdrawn," *Science* 277 (July 25, 1997): 462–63. For reference to additional research results challenging the thesis of diminished fertility due to environmental hormones see Stephen Safe, "Another Enviro-Scare Debunked," *Wall Street Journal*, August 20, 1997, p. A14.

48. Jessica Mathews, "Overlooking the 'POPs' Problem," *Washington Post*, March 11, 1996, p. A19.

49. Paul Connett, "The Third Citizens' Conference on Dioxin and Other Synthetic Hormone Disrupters," *IEN Network News* 3 (Late Summer 1996), p. 14.

50. Environmental Protection Agency, *Environmental Equity: Reducing Risk for All Communities—Volume 1: Workgroups Report to the Administrator* (Washington, D.C.: June 1992), p. 3.

51. Ibid.

52. Ibid., *Volume 2: Supporting Documents*, p. 9. See also Centers for Disease Control, ATSDR, *The Nature and Extent of Lead Poisoning in Children in the United States: A Report to Congress* (Atlanta: Centers for Disease Control, 1988).

53. Testimony of Victor J. Kimm, deputy assistant administrator, Office of Prevention, Pesticides, and Toxic Substances, EPA, in, *Lead Poisoning* (Hearing before the House Subcommittee on health and the environment), 102d Cong., 2d sess., February 25, 1992, (GPO, 1992) pt. 2, p. 107.

54. Peter Samuel, "Weighing the Worries over Lead," *Washington Times*, November 15, 1995, p. A12.

55. *Lead Poisoning (Part 2)*, hearing, p. 112.

56. See Kathryn R. Mahaffey, "Exposure to Lead in Childhood: The Importance of Prevention," *New England Journal of Medicine* 327 (October 29, 1992): 1308–1309; Peter A. Baghurst et. al., "Environmental Exposure to Lead and Children's Intelligence at the Age of Seven Years—The Port Pirie Cohort Study," *New England Journal of Medicine* 327 (Ocotober 29, 1992): 1279–1284; Jane E. Brody, "Aggressiveness and Delinquency in Boys is Linked to Lead in Bones," *New York Times* (February 7, 1996), p. C9. For criticism of this research, and of the uses to which advocates have put it, see: Peter Samuel, "Weighing the Worries Over Lead," *The Washington Times*, November 15, 1995, p. A112; Sandra Scarr, "Science, Public Policy, and a Critic's Dilemma," *PSR Quarterly* 3 (March 1993): 27–31; and Ellen Ruppel Shell, "An Element of Doubt," *The Atlantic Monthly* (December 1995): 24, 26, 28, 36, 38, 39.

57. Matthew L. Wald, "Lead Paint: New Rules Announced," *New York Times*, March 7, 1996, p. C12.

58. Albert L. Nichols, "Risk-Based Priorities and Environmental Justice," in Adam M. Finkel and Dominic Golding, eds., *Worst Things First? The Debate over Risk-Based National Environmental Priorities* (Washington, D.C.: Resources for the Future, 1994), pp. 269–70. A detailed case study of the leaded gasoline phasedown is George M. Gray, Laury Saligman, and John D. Graham, "The Demise of Lead in Gasoline," in John D. Graham and Jennifer Kassalow Hartwell, eds., *The Greening of Industry: A Risk Management Approach* (Cambridge, Mass.: Harvard University Press, 1997), pp. 17–41.

59. "Unleaded, Please," (segment of statistical compilation entitled "What on Earth? A Weekly Look at Trends, People and Events Around the World") *Washington Post*, July 5, 1997, p. A22.

60. An extensive criticism of national lead removal policy is Cassandra Chrones Moore, *Haunted Housing: How Toxic Scare Stories Are Spooking the Public Out of House and Home* (Washington, D.C.: Cato Institute, 1997), ch. 2.

61. The statute is the Federal Insecticide, Fungicide and Rodenticide Act (FIFRA). See Christopher J. Bosso, *Pesticides and Politics: The Life Cycle of a Public Issue* (Pittsburgh: University of Pittsburgh Press, 1987).

62. See Baldemar Velasquez testimony in Environmental Protection Agency, *A National Dialogue on the Worker Protection Standard—Part I: Transcripts of the Public Meetings* (EPA 735-R97-001) (Washington, D.C., March 1997), pp. 17–19.

63. Ivette Perfecto, "Pesticide Exposure of Farm Workers and the International Connection," in Bunyan Bryant and Paul Mohai, eds., *Race and the Incidence of Environmental Hazards: A Time for Discourse* (Boulder, Colo.: Westview Press, 1992), pp. 180–81.

64. See 57 *Federal Register* (August 21, 1992): 38102–76; 60 *Federal Register* (May 3, 1995): 21944–68; and 60 *Federal Register* (September 29, 1995): 50682–91.

65. 60 *Federal Register* (May 3, 1995): 21960.

66. Author's notes from May 1996 NEJAC meeting.

67. On asthma generally see: Geoffrey Cowley and Anne Underwood, "Why Ebonie Can't Breathe," *Newsweek* (May 26, 1997), pp. 58–64; Ken Flieger, "Controlling Asthma," *FDA Consumer* (November 1996) (electronic copy at *www.fda.gov/fdac/features/996/_asth.html*); American Lung Association, *Lung Disease in Minorities 1998* (Washington, D.C., 1998), pp. 3–4; Sally Squires, "New Attack on Asthma," *Washington Post Health*, April 15, 1997, pp. Z12–14, 16; David L. Rosenstreich, et al., "The Role of Cockroach Allergy and Exposure to Cockroach Allergen in Causing Morbidity Among Inner-City Children with Asthma," *New England Journal of Medicine* 336 (May 8, 1997): 1356–63; and Thomas A E. Platts-Mills, and Melody C. Carter, "Asthma and Indoor Exposure to Allergens," *New England Journal of Medicine* 336 (May 8, 1997): 1382–84.

68. American Lung Association, *Minority Lung Disease Data 1996*, p. 3.

69. Rosenstreich, et al, "The Role of Cockroach Allergy," p. 1356.

70. Ibid.

71. Council on Environmental Quality, *Environmental Quality: The Second Annual Report of the Council on Environmental Quality* (August 1971), ch. 6.

72. See, for example: Michael Specter, "Seeing Risk Everywhere: In Epidemic of Fear, Major Threats Ignored," *Washington Post*, May 7, 1989, pp. A1, A20; Peter Passell, "Life's Risks: Balancing Fear Against Reality of Statistics," *New York Times*, May 8, 1989, pp. A1, D12; Daniel Goleman, "Hidden Rules Often Distort Ideas of Risk," *New York Times*, February 1, 1994, pp. C1, C10; and Environmental Protection Agency, *Unfinished Business: A Comparative Assessment of Environmental Problems—Overview Report* (Washington, D.C.: February 1987), p. xv.

73. Howard Margolis, *Dealing with Risk: Why the Public and the Experts Disagree on Environmental Issues* (University of Chicago Press, 1996), p. 21, emphasis in original.

74. See Margolis, ch. 2.

75. Ibid, p. 22.

76. Ibid, p. 71.

77. Ibid, p. 88.

78. As Margolis describes the findings of social psychology, "willingness to pay for a very small increment to safety is usually near zero *except* when that small increment is the last increment." Ibid., p. 83, emphasis in original.

79. Ibid, p. 82.

80. This author once encountered his own intuitive limitations quite abruptly as a student. I wondered for most of an introductory physics lecture how it could be that a bullet's forward velocity remains independent of its downward fall due to gravity. Professor Costas Papaliolios of the Harvard physics department convincingly demonstrated that which had seemed to me very unlikely.

81. Gina Kolata, "Could It Be? Weather Has Nothing to Do with Your Arthritis Pain?" *New York Times* April 3, 1996, p. C 13.

82. Adam Nossiter, "Villain Is Dioxin. Relocation Is Response. But Judgment Is in Dispute" *New York Times,* October 21, 1996, p. A12. The relocation campaign may have succeeded largely because of political sensitivities, not analysis. Observers noted that the EPA's decision came shortly before the 1996 presidential election, in a state that a Democratic president was especially anxious to win, and where he could win only with a strongly supportive minority electorate. Even if presidential campaign politics played no role, it seems clear that the EPA's decision to grant relocation assistance was controversial within the agency on risk grounds and that the minority status of the Escambia community was a significant consideration. See also Michael Gough, "EPA's Sham Science Reveals Political Agenda," *Regulation* (Winter 1997): 15–16.

83. Julia Preston, "Pots That Poison, and Potters Facing Broken Lives," *New York Times,* June 14, 1996, p. A4.

84. Mirta Ojito, "Ritual Use of Mercury Prompts Testing of Children for Illness," *New York Times,* December 14, 1997, pp. 53–54.

85. Foreman, *Plagues, Products and Politics,* ch. 3.

86. Kate Darby Rauch, "The Spiritual Use of Poisonous Mercury," *Washington Post Health,* August 13, 1991, p. 7; Arnold P. Wendroff, "Magico-Religious Mercury Use and Cultural Sensitivity," *American Journal of Public Health* 85 (March 1995): 409–10. The author wishes to thank Arnold P. Wendroff of the Mercury Poisoning Project in Brooklyn, New York, for access to some of the voluminous materials he has collected on this subject.

87. David Lewis Feldman, Ralph Perhac, and Ruth Anne Hanahan, *Environmental Priority-Setting in U.S. States and Communities: A Comparative Analysis* (Knoxville, Tenn.: Energy, Environment and Resources Center, University of Tennessee, September 1996). This research found that the vast majority of state comparative risk projects embraced the EPA's three prescribed categories of risk: human health, ecosystem health, and quality of life.

Chapter 5

1. Although as noted in the previous chapter, "collective bads" like dirty air and undrinkable water tend to impose costs on everyone in the vicinity, regardless of income.

2. Martha Derthick, *Policymaking for Social Security* (Washington, D.C.: The Brookings Institution, 1979), p. 3.

3. Christopher H. Foreman, Jr., *Signals from the Hill: Congressional Oversight and the Challenge of Social Regulation* (Yale University Press, 1988), pp. 175–76.

4. Curtis Moore and Alan Miller, *Green Gold: Japan, Germany, the United States, and the Race for Environmental Technology* (Boston: Beacon Press, 1994).

5. James Q. Wilson, *Bureaucracy: What Government Agencies Do and Why They Do It* (New York: Basic Books, 1989), ch. 4.

6. House of Representatives, Committee on the Judiciary, *Environmental Justice* (Hearings before the Subcommittee on Civil and Constitutional Rights), 103rd Cong., 1st sess., March 3 and 4, 1993, p. 18.

7. Americans, black and white, remain overwhelmingly supportive of job training as an affirmative action approach. A December 1997 *New York Times*/CBS News Poll of support for affirmative action among blacks and whites asked respondents whether they favored "government financing for job training for minorities to help them get ahead in industries where they are underrepresented [such as environmental remediation]." Almost two-thirds of whites (64 percent) and *95 percent of blacks* (the largest percentage reported for any response by any category of respondent) favored such financing. Sam Howe Verhovek, "In Poll, Americans Reject Means But Not Ends of Racial Diversity," *New York Times*, December 14, 1997, pp. 1, 34.

8. Jonathan Lash, Katherine Gillman, and David Sheridan, *A Season of Spoils: The Reagan Administration's Attack on the Environment* (New York: Pantheon Books, 1984).

9. Charles Bartsch and Elizabeth Collaton, *Coming Clean for Economic Development: A Resource Book on Environmental Cleanup and Economic Development* (Washington, D.C.: Northeast-Midwest Institute, 1996), p. 8.

10. Ibid.

11. For example, one source notes that Detroit alone has some 2,500 or more "abandoned, possibly polluted sites." *Atlantic Siteline* (Colchester, Conn.: Atlantic Environmental Services, February 1996), p. 1.

12. The material in this paragraph is taken from EPA, Office of Solid Waste and Emergency Response, Office of Outreach and Special Projects, "Brownfields Pilots" (EPA-500-F-96-001), dated June 1996.

13. Up-to-date information on the growing number of Brownfields Assessment Demonstration Pilots can be found on the EPA website at *www.epa.gov/swerosps/bf/pilot.htm*.

14. The latter figure was offered by EPA administrator Carol Browner during April 1996 congressional testimony. See House of Representatives, Committee on Appropriations, *Departments of Veterans Affairs and Housing and Urban Development, and Independent Agencies Appropriations for 1997—Part 5: Environmental Protection Agency* (hearings before a subcommittee) 104th Cong., 2d sess. (1996), p. 43.

15. See Bartsch and Collaton, *Coming Clean for Economic Development*, and Edith M. Pepper, *Lessons from the Field: Unlocking Economic Potential with an Environmental Key* (Washington, D.C.: Northeast-Midwest Institute, 1997).

16. See Environmental Protection Agency, *Environmental Justice, Urban Revitalization, and Brownfields: The Search for Authentic Signs of Hope—A Report on the Public Dialogues on Urban Revitalization and Brownfields: Envisioning Healthy and Sustainable Communities* (December 1996).

17. See Bennett Harrison with Marcus Weiss and Jon Gant, *Building Bridges: Community Development Corporations and the World of Employment Training* (New York: Ford Foundation, January 1995); Bennett Harrison and Amy K. Glasmeier, "Response: Why Business Alone Won't Redevelop the Inner City: A Friendly Critique of Michael Porter's Approach to Urban Revitalization," *Economic Development Quarterly* 11 (February 1997): 28–38; and Avis C. Vidal, "CDCs as Agents of Neighborhood Change: The State of the Art," in W. Dennis Keating, Norman Krumholz, and Philip Star, eds., *Revitalizing Urban Neighborhoods* (Lawrence: University Press of Kansas, 1996), pp. 149–63. On the Ford Foundation's role see Richard Moe and Carter Wilkie, *Changing Places: Rebuilding Community in the Age of Sprawl* (New York: Henry Holt, 1997), pp. 140–41.

18. Michael E. Porter, "New Strategies for Inner-City Economic Development," *Economic Development Quarterly* 11 (February 1997): 11–27. See also Michael E. Porter, "The Competitive Advantage of the Inner City," *Harvard Business Review* 73 (May–June 1995): 55–71.

19. See Harrison and Glasmeier, "Response," and Timothy Bates, "Response: Michael Porter's Conservative Urban Agenda Will Not Revitalize America's Inner Cities: What Will?" *Economic Development Quarterly* 11 (February 1997): 39–44.

20. This section is based heavily on discussion with Steve Fenton, associate director of HMTRI. See also Steve Fenton and Michael Senew, "Community Colleges Play an Important Role in EPA's Brownfields Economic Redevelopment Initiative," *ATEEC News* 3 (Winter 1997): 3–4.

21. See *http://www.htmri.org/htmri-g3.htm#C3*.

22. Fenton and Senew, "Community Colleges Play an Important Role," p. 3.

23. See National Institute of Environmental Health Sciences, *Environmental Job Training for Inner City Youth: Report of the Technical Workshop January 5–6, 1995 Cuyahoga Community College, Cleveland, Ohio* (April 17, 1995), p. 4.

24. NIEHS, *Environmental Job Training for Inner City Youth*, p. 4.

25. Quoted in ibid., Appendix 6.

26. Ibid.

27. NIEHS, "National Institute of Environmental Health Sciences Announces the Recipients of the Minority Worker Training Program Cooperative Agreements," dated November 10, 1995.

28 See, for example, Robert D. Bullard and Beverly Hendrix Wright, "The Politics of Pollution: Implications for the Black Community. *Phylon* 47 (March 1986): 71–78.

29. Environmental Protection Agency, Office of Emergency and Remedial Response, " The Superfund Jobs Training Initiative (SuperJTI)," December 1996.

30. Ibid.

31. W. Kip Viscusi, *Risk by Choice: Regulating Health and Safety in the Workplace* (Cambridge, Mass.: Harvard University Press, 1983).

32. NIEHS, *Environmental Job Training for Inner City Youth*, p. 15

33. Ibid., p. 22.

34. Ibid.

35. Ibid., p. 26.

36. Ibid.

37. See, for example, Laurie J. Bassi and Orley Ashenfelter, "The Effect of Direct Job Creation and Training Programs on Low-Skilled Workers," in Sheldon H. Danziger and Daniel H. Weinberg, eds., *Fighting Poverty: What Works and What Doesn't* (Cambridge, Mass.: Harvard University Press, 1986), pp. 133–51; Nathan Glazer, "Education and Training Programs and Poverty," in Danziger and Weinberg, eds., *Fighting Poverty*, pp. 152–73; Roberta M. Blank, "The Employment Strategy: Public Policies to Increase Work and Earnings," in Sheldon H. Danziger, Gary D. Sandefur, Daniel H. Weinberg, eds., *Confronting Poverty: Prescriptions for Change* (Cambridge, Mass.: Harvard University Press and New York: Russell Sage Foundation, 1994), pp. 168–204; W. Norton Grubb, *Learning to Work: The Case for Reintegrating Job Training and Education* (New York: Russell Sage Foundation, 1996); and Robert I. Lerman, "Building Hope, Skills and Careers: Creating a Youth Apprenticeship System," in Irwin Garfinkel, Jennifer L. Hochschild, and Sara S. McLanahan, eds., *Social Policies for Children* (Washington, D.C.: Brookings Institution, 1996), pp. 136–72. A notably optimistic assessment of prospects for employment training is Harrison, Weiss, and Gant, *Building Bridges: Community Development Corporations and the World of Employment Training* (New York: Ford Foundation, 1995).

38. Blank, "The Employment Strategy," p. 190.

39. Ibid., p. 191.

40. Lerman, "Building Hope, Skills and Careers," p. 141.

41. Grubb, *Learning to Work*, p. 6.

42. William Julius Wilson, "Public Policy Research and The Truly Disadvantaged," in Christopher Jencks and Paul E. Peterson, eds., *The Urban Underclass* (Washington, D.C.: The Brookings Institution, 1991), pp. 460–81. See

also Nicholas Lemann, "The Myth of Community Development," *New York Times Magazine*, January 9, 1994, pp. 27–35.

43. William Julius Wilson, *When Work Disappears: The World of the New Urban Poor* (New York: Alfred A. Knopf, 1996), p. 224.

44 Ibid.

45. Ibid., p. 228. See also Edward M. Gramlich, "The Main Themes," in Danziger and Weinberg, eds., *Fighting Poverty*, pp. 343–44.

46. Henry Payne, "'Environmental Justice' Kills Jobs for the Poor," *Wall Street Journal*, September 16, 1997, p. A22.

Chapter 6

1. On general economic critiques of regulation during the Reagan era see Robert E. Litan and William D. Nordhaus, *Reforming Federal Regulation* (New Haven and London: Yale University Press, 1983), and George C. Eads and Michael Fix, *Relief or Reform? Reagan's Regulatory Dilemma* (Washington, D.C.: Urban Institute Press, 1984). A recent examination of the uses and limitations of economic analysis at the EPA is Richard D. Morgenstern, ed., *Economic Analyses at EPA: Assessing Regulatory Impact* (Washington, D.C.: Resources for the Future, 1997). The most significant incentive-based approach to environmental regulation yet adopted is a system of tradable emission allowances for sulfur dioxide created by the Clean Air Act of 1990. See Gary C. Bryner, *Blue Skies, Green Politics: The Clean Air Act of 1990 and Its Implementation* (Washington, D.C.: Congressional Quarterly Press, 1995), pp. 169–73.

2. Stephen Breyer, *Breaking the Vicious Circle: Toward Effective Risk Regulation* (Cambridge, Mass.: Harvard University Press, 1993), ch. 1.

3. Ibid., p. 11.

4. Ibid., p. 17.

5. Ibid., pp. 59–60.

6. Committee for the National Institute for the Environment, *A Proposal for a National Institute for the Environment: Need, Rationale, and Structure* (Washington, D.C., September 1993), p. 1. As the executive summary of the proposal argues: "The nation needs a new paradigm for organizing and guiding environmental research, and for integrating research findings with timely and comprehensive assessments of the state of knowledge. It needs a means of communicating credible information about the environment, and of ensuring that higher education and training meet national needs for environmental expertise. The key to success is bringing these functions together in a single home where they can interact and mutually support each other."

7. John Wargo, *Our Children's Toxic Legacy: How Science and Law Fail to Protect Us from Pesticides* (New Haven and London: Yale University Press, 1996), p. 292.

8. Critical overviews of the antiscientific, even antirational thinking common in academia include Paul R. Gross and Norman Levitt, *Higher Superstition: The Academic Left and Its Quarrels with Science* (Baltimore and London: Johns Hopkins University Press, 1994), and Paul R. Gross, Norman Levitt, and Martin W. Lewis, eds., *The Flight from Science and Reason* (New York: New York Academy of Sciences, 1996).

9. Andrew Szasz, *EcoPopulism: Toxic Waste and the Movement for Environmental Justice* (Minneapolis and London: University of Minnesota Press, 1994), p. 82.

10. Bunyan Bryant, "Introduction," in Bunyan Bryant, ed., *Environmental Justice: Issues, Policies and Solutions* (Washington, D.C. and Covelo, Calif.: Island Press, 1995), p. 5.

11. Szasz, p. 81.

12. Ibid.

13. Lois Gibbs and the Citizens Clearinghouse for Hazardous Waste, *Dying from Dioxin: A Citizen's Guide to Reclaiming Our Health and Rebuilding Democracy* (Boston: South End Press, 1995), pp. 189–90.

14. Linda King, "Health Studies: Can They Help or Hurt Organizing Efforts?" *Indigenous Environmental Network News* (Late Summer 1996): 10.

15. Richard A. Harris and Sidney M. Milkis, *The Politics of Regulatory Change: A Tale of Two Agencies* (New York and Oxford: Oxford University Pres, 1989). On Sidney Wolfe of the Health Research Group, see Susan Okie, "Running on Outrage," *Washington Post Health*, December 5, 1989, pp. 12–15.

16. See for example Bunyan Bryant, "Issues and Potential Policies and Solutions for Environmental Justice: An Overview," in Bryant, ed., *Environmental Justice*, pp. 8–34.

17. Cindy F. Kleiman, "Scientific Peer Review and Conflict of Interest," 9 *Priorities* 1 (1997): 33.

18. Walter A Rosenbaum, *Environmental Politics and Policy*, 3rd ed. (Washington, D.C.: Congressional Quarterly Press, 1995), p. 141.

19. Recent research indicates similar difficulty among states and communities pursuing comparative risk projects. Phase I of such projects (in which risks are identified, characterized, and ranked) appears to have a hard time generating a reallocation of resources in the subsequent risk management phase "because of the potential political costs entailed in alienating constituencies and/or threatening established programs." David Lewis Feldman, Ruth Anne Hanahan, and Ralph Perhac, *Subnational Comparative Risk Projects: An Analysis of Their Risk Management Phase* (Knoxville, Tenn.: Energy, Environment and Resources Center, University of Tennessee, September 1997), p. 28.

20. Robert D. Bullard, "Unequal Environmental Protection: Incorporating Environmental Justice in Decision Making," in Adam M. Finkel and Dominic

Golding, eds., *Worst Things First? The Debate over Risk-Based National Environmental Priorities* (Washington, D.C.: Resources for the Future, 1994), p. 259.

21. Ibid.

22. Associated Press, "Cigarette Campaign Denounced. Scrap Drive Aimed at Blacks, Health Secretary Says," *Chicago Tribune* January 19, 1990, p. 1; Anthony Ramirez, "Reynolds, After Protests, Cancels Cigarette Aimed at Black Smokers," *New York Times*, January 20, 1990, p. 1; Janet Cawley, "Fired Up," *Chicago Tribune*, April 16, 1990, p. 1.

23. Albert L. Nichols, "Risk-Based Priorities and Environmental Justice," in Finkel and Golding, eds., *Worst Things First?* p. 268, emphasis in original.

24. A systematic exploration of risk tradeoffs is John D. Graham and Jonathan Baert Wiener, eds., *Risk vs. Risk: Tradeoffs in Protecting Health and the Environment* (Cambridge, Mass.: Harvard University Press, 1995).

25. Telephone interview, March 12, 1996.

26. See Robert Bullard, "Environmental Blackmail in Minority Communities," in Bunyan Bryant and Paul Mohai, eds., *Race and the Incidence of Environmental Hazards: A Time for Discourse* (Boulder, Colo.: Westview Press, 1992), pp. 82–95, and also Bryant and Mohai, "Introduction," in Bryant and Mohai, eds., *Race and the Incidence of Environmental Hazards*, p. 2.

27. See, for example, Robert D. Bullard, "Anatomy of Environmental Racism and the Environmental Justice Movement," in Bullard, ed., *Confronting Environmental Racism: Voices from the Grassroots* (Boston: South End Press, 1993), p. 21, and Regina Austin and Michael Schill, "Black, Brown, Red, and Poisoned," in Bullard, ed., *Unequal Protection: Environmental Justice and Communities of Color* (San Francisco: Sierra Club Books, 1994), p. 61.

28. Martin V. Melosi, "Equity, Eco-Racism and Environmental History," *Environmental History Review* 19 (Fall 1995): 10.

29. William Claiborne, "CIA Chief Faces Angry Crowd at Los Angeles Meeting on Drug Allegations," *Washington Post*, November 16, 1986, p. A6.

30. On the Tuskegee syphilis study, see John F. Harris and Michael A. Fletcher, "Six Decades Later, An Apology; Saying 'I Am Sorry,' President Calls Tuskegee Experiment 'Shameful.'" *Washington Post*, May 17, 1997, p. A1. See also James H. Jones, *Bad Blood: The Tuskegee Syphilis Experiment* (New York: Free Press, 1993).

31. Senior officials in the Clinton EPA will almost certainly beg to differ on this point. But however committed even they may be as individuals to environmental justice, two compelling realities remain. First, EPA's primary statutory framework remains utterly silent on the matter. Nor has the judiciary filled the void. Second, environmental justice advocacy comprises only a tiny fraction of the total lobbying effort and political pressure directed toward the agency.

32. See Gibbs and the Citizens Clearinghouse for Hazardous Waste, *Dying from Dioxin*, p. xxiii.

33. Ibid., p. 146.

34. Thomas Lambert and Christopher Boerner, "Environmental Inequity: Economic Causes, Economic Solutions," *Yale Journal on Regulation* 14 (Winter 1997): 195–234.

35. Barry G. Rabe, *Beyond NIMBY: Hazardous Waste Siting in Canada and the United States* (Washington, D.C.: Brookings Institution, 1994).

36. Robert D. Bullard, J. Eugene Grigsby III, and Charles Lee, eds., *Residential Apartheid: The American Legacy* (Los Angeles: CAAS Publications, 1994). For a good examination of the complexities (including minority residential preferences) that govern residential housing patterns, see Stephan Thernstrom and Abigail Thernstrom, *America in Black and White: One Nation, Indivisible* (New York: Simon and Schuster, 1997), ch. 8.

37. John H. Cushman Jr., "Efficient Pollution Rule Under Attack," *New York Times*, June 28, 1995, p. A16. See also Robert Gottlieb, Maureen Smith, Julie Roque, and Pamela Yates, "New Approaches to Toxics: Production Design, Right-to-Know, and Definition Debates," in Robert Gottlieb, ed., *Reducing Toxics: A New Approach to Policy and Industrial Decisionmaking* (Washington, D.C., and Covelo, Calif.: Island Press, 1995), pp. 124–65. On the limitations of TRI as an indicator of overall releases see Mark Atlas, "Inaccuracy in Pollutant Emission Data: TRI, TRI Again," (unpublished paper, Carnegie Mellon University, 1995).

38. See for example Bryant, pp. 21–23.

39. See, for example, Office of Pollution Prevention and Toxics, *Environmental Justice Through Pollution Prevention Grant Guidance 1995* (Washington, D.C.: EPA, 1994). For a brief analysis and critique of the Pollution Prevention Act of 1990 see Gottlieb, Smith, Roque, and Yates, "New Approaches to Toxics," pp. 130–31.

40. Melosi, "Equity, Eco-Racism and Environmental History," p. 11.

41. Animal and Plant Health Inspection Service, *Lower Rio Grande Valley Boll Weevil Eradication Program: Final Assessment* (Riverdale, Md.: Department of Agriculture, March 1995), p. 16.

42. Sam Howe Verhovek, "Racial Rift Slows Suit for 'Environmental Justice,'" *New York Times*, September 7, 1997, pp. 1, 32. See also Christopher H. Foreman Jr., "Down in the Dumps—On Purpose," *Washington Times*, November 4, 1997, p. A21.

43. "Accusations of Racism Halt a Nuclear Plant," *Washington Post*, May 4, 1997, p. A4. See also Nuclear Regulatory Commission, Atomic Safety and Licensing Board, *Final Initial Decision—Louisiana Energy Services* Docket No. 70-3070-ML, dated May 1, 1997.

44. "LES Withdraws License Application," *LLWnotes* vol. 13, no. 3 (April 1998), p. 3.

45. Letter to the author from Brooke Barnes, enforcement officer, Maine Department of Environmental Protection, March 17, 1995. Letter to the author dated March 13, 1995, from Katherine J. Orr, chief legal counsel, Montana Department of Health and Environmental Sciences. Letter to the author dated March 13, 1995, from J. R. Sandoval, assistant administrator, Division of Environmental Quality, Idaho Department of Health and Welfare.

46. Letter to the author dated March 14, 1995, from Daniel H. Thompson, deputy secretary, Florida Department of Environmental Protection.

47. Fawn Johnson, undated memo to the author; based on telephone conversation with Clyde Pike of the Texas Natural Resources Conservation Commission.

48. Louisiana Advisory Committee to the U.S. Commission on Civil Rights, *The Battle for Environmental Justice in Louisiana . . . Government, Industry, and the People* (September 1993), and Louisiana Department of Environmental Quality, *Final Report to the Louisiana Legislature on Environmental Justice* (August 24, 1994).

49. *Oregon Environmental Equity Citizen Advisory Committee Report: A Report to the Governor on Ensuring Environmental Equity in Oregon* (October 1994).

50. Peter T. Kilborn, "Health Gap Grows, with Black Americans Trailing Whites, Studies Say," *New York Times* January, 26, 1998, A16.

51. David Lewis Feldman, Ralph Perhac, and Ruth Anne Hanahan, *Environmental Priority-Setting in U.S. States and Communities: A Comparative Analysis* (Knoxville, Tenn.: Energy, Environment and Resources Center, University of Tennessee, September 1996), p. vi. It is worth noting that the last of these concerns—fairness to future generations—recalls yet another rubric widely criticized for vagueness: sustainability. See Ian Hodge, *Environmental Economics: Individual Incentives and Public Choices* (New York: St. Martin's Press, 1995), p. 52.

52. Office of Policy, Planning and Evaluation, *A Guidebook to Comparing Risks and Setting Environmental Priorities*, EPA 230-B-93-003 (Washington, D.C.: EPA, September 1993), section 2.4.

53. George L. Kelling and James Q. Wilson, "Broken Windows," *Atlantic Monthly* (March 1982), pp. 29–36.

54. In a 1984 analysis for the California Waste Management Board, Cerrell Associates advised that "middle and higher socioeconomic strata neighborhoods should not fall within the one-mile and five-mile radius of the proposed site" for a facility because such neighborhoods "possess better resources to effectuate their opposition." Quoted in Robert Bullard, "Residential Segregation and Urban Quality of Life," in Bryant, ed., *Environmental Justice*, p. 78. The activist literature generally treats this report as a kind of "smoking gun" regarding the deliberate intent to burden low-income minority communities that are less likely to resist polluting facilities. But the questions of what is in any given community's interest, and of what constitutes a threat to that

interest, is a matter that must elude prejudgments grounded in presumptions of unacceptable risk.

55. Richard Moe and Cater Wilkie, *Changing Places: Rebuilding Community in the Age of Sprawl* (New York: Henry Holt and Co., 1997), ch. 2.

56. As Moe and Wilkie recount: "To measure the suitability of a location for mortgage insurance, the FHA looked first and foremost for serious threats to future property values: evidence of blight and decay and any signs of African Americans or other racial or ethnic groups who might not suit a potential buyer's preference for all-white neighborhoods. A single house occupied by a black family in an urban neighborhood, even one tucked away on an inconspicuous side street, was enough for the FHA to label a predominantly white neighborhood as unfit for mortgage insurance." Ibid., p. 48.

57. Ibid., p. 139.

58. On the Chicago-area Gatreaux relocation program and the U.S. Department of Housing and Urban Development's Moving to Opportunity for Fair Housing Demonstration (MTO) see Jens Ludwig and Simeon Stolzberg, "HUD's Moving to Opportunity Demonstration: Uncertain Benefits, Unlikely Costs, Unfortunate Politics," *Georgetown Public Policy Review* 1 (1995): 25–37, and Orlando Patterson, *The Ordeal of Integration: Progress and Resentment in America's "Racial" Crisis* (Washington, D.C.: Civitas/Counterpoint, 1997), ch. 1.

59. Robert Halpern, *Rebuilding the Inner City: A History of Neighborhood Initiatives to Address Poverty in the United States* (New York: Columbia University Press, 1995), p. 4.

60. Lambert and Boerner, "Environmental Inequity: Economic Causes, Economic Solutions," pp. 227–28.

61. See, for example, Patrick C. West, "Invitation to Poison? Detroit Minorities and Toxic Fish Consumption from the Detroit River," and Patrick C. West, J. Mark Fly, Frances Larkin, and Robert C. Marans, "Minority Anglers and Toxic Fish Consumption: Evidence from a Statewide Survey of Michigan," in Bryant and Mohai, eds., *Race and the Incidence of Environmental Hazards*, pp. 96–113. But see also Paul D. Anderson and Jonathan Baert Wiener, "Eating Fish," in Graham and Wiener, eds., *Risk vs. Risk*, pp. 104–23.

62. Vincent T. Covello, David B. McCallum, and Maria T. Pavlova, eds., *Effective Risk Communication: The Role and Responsibility of Government and Nongovernment Organizations* (New York: Plenum Press, 1989).

63. Environmental justice proponents are often suspicious of behavioral approaches to health as an excuse to "blame the victim." For example, Bunyan Bryant writes: "Often research findings and health care policies assign blame for sickness at the individual rather than the institutional level. Health care policies are intended to help people make the right choices in order to live healthy lives despite the fact that they may live in contaminated communities. Disseminating information for people to make informed health care choices is part of the

rugged individualism that grew out of the pioneering spirit of this country. The ideology of individualism blames the victims—not the polluting institutions. If a person becomes ill, it is because they made bad choices or failed to take care of themselves. The ideology of individualism not only blames victims for their toxic-induced and aggravated illnesses, but also keeps people from confronting institutions that may have created the condition for their illness in the first place." See Bryant, p. 17.

64. Elizabeth Whelan, "Be Afraid of Smoking," *Weekly Standard*, June 16, 1997, p. 7.

65. Barbara M. Dixon with Josleen Wilson, *Good Health for African Americans* (New York: Crown Trade Paperbacks, 1994), pp. 75–77, and Michael Fumento, *The Fat of the Land: The Obesity Epidemic and How Overweight Americans Can Help Themselves* (New York: Viking, 1997), chs. 1, 2, and p. 127.

INDEX